LIFE Out LOUD

with Mike McClure Sr.

www.TrueVinePublishing.org

Life Out Loud with Mike McClure, Sr.
Dr. Mike McClure, Sr.

Published by
True Vine Publishing Co.
P.O. Box 22448
Nashville, TN. 37202
www.TrueVinePublishing.org

ISBN: 978-1-956469-00-4 Paperback
ISBN: 978-1-956469-11-0 eBook

Printed in the United States of America—First Printing

DEDICATION

I write this first book in dedication to the love of my life and my life's greatest friend and cheerleader, my wife and mother of all three of my children, Angela W. McClure.

Thank you, Angie, for always believing in me and my dreams, always speaking life, sending love and sharing laughter with your boy! Thanks for my three treasured gifts Mike, Jr., (Jaquetta) Dee (Brittany) & Slim. Without you all in my life I really can't fathom life as I've come to know and enjoy it. I love, learn, love, lead, and laugh out loud because you are forever in my head and my heart saying, "You got this!"!

Thanks for all the good times! I love you

Foreword

I'm Flynn Johnson. I've been sleeping with my wife for 50 years and we've been in ministry for more than 45 years together. We pastor a local church in the Greatest city in the world – Atlanta Georgia. I lead an international apostolic company of pastors and leaders of which Mike and Angela have been members for over 30 years. I am proud to say, he is my son in the Gospel. We are extremely proud of how he has lead his entire family in ministry – which is a miraculous feat in this culture's climate.

I was introduced to Mike McClure by a spiritual son who recognized Mike's hunger for God's presence and power. When we met, immediately I knew he was a live wire. I mean this guy was "all the way lit." He was loud, boisterous, and brassy, yet humble all at the same time. My wife's description of him however is not appropriate to say here. We'll just say, "Mike McClure was a piece of work." I liked him immediately.

He was always a quick study, an avid reader, a top-notch learner. As soon as he understood what God was saying He began to implement it. Over the years I watched his ministry increase as his influence expanded. Mike is a loving leader who I've traveled and worked with for several years. It's been fun to watch how his ministry impacts the lives of others; especially those who are torn and broken. I'm amazed at the number of men and women whose lives have been snatched from the brink of darkness because of

Mike's word and ministry. And not just those of his local church, but also those who are leading other ministries. They look to him for answers, for direction. Surely, they see him as an example.

As my wife, Carolyn and I have ministered to couples and families for so many years, we have no better couple to team with than Mike and Angela. As a team member, I have depended on Mike to say things to some leaders that I don't say well. His word and his humor are convicting, inspiring, entertaining and life changing. This is a good description of this book. It's why the reader should take it slow and allow each chapter to have its impact on their life. Today, we need to hear from those who walk the talk; not those who merely squawk.

We need a word that comes in real flesh and blood. Mike **lives** from the inside out, He's not afraid to show his feelings. He's always been a straight shooter. Mike is constantly **learning** so He can impart to others. He **loves** others even to his own hurt. I've seen him be gracious and forgiving to others even when they deserved the opposite. Mike **leads** by example. I've never seen him ask others to do what he himself has not or is not doing. If he gets it wrong, he repents and asks for forgiveness; especially those he leads. I have come to learn that when Mike **laughs** the loudest, he's hurting the most. But that's the weapon he's wheels to overcome his enemies.

To say the least, this book is the epitome of who Mike is. He **Learns** daily to impart to others. He **loves**, even when he's hurting, he **leads** those who actually follow. Mike **Laughs** despite difficultly, defeat, and downfalls. And Michael McClure **Lends** phenomenally. He is one of the most generous persons I know.

In the pages of this book Mike opens his life, as he always does with transparency, brutal honesty. His insightful wisdom is a true testament of his own self-awareness as he has well lived each lesson. His Biblical applications are a good refresher. If you knew him, you'd know that he intends the results of this book to be a Grand introduction to God's Provision in your life.

This book goes out to anyone who is in or out of leadership. It's for those who feel like their dreams are dead, or on a ventilator. These words are for those who lead but have recently discovered they're only taking a walk. Mike writes for those who speak at a whisper or who's mouths are shut for fear of negative confrontation, or **rejection**. If you are a cold and timid soul who has tapped out because of the pain that would not dare allow you to give another thing to anyone; especially themselves. This is for you! And to those who carry so much sorrow, they've forgotten the power of the corners of their lips stretch from one ear to the next; this is just the read you need. Mike will deliver exactly what you need with holiness and hilarity.

This is for **Leaders** who **Live** in glass houses that are **Learning** to **Love, Laugh** and
Lend again!

Bishop Flynn A. Johnson

Contents

INTRODUCTION

Allow me to first introduce you to this journey through the pages of my life with an all-inclusive disclaimer. Ready? Here it is: "The only thing I've ever perfected in my life is LIVING my life freely!"

This is not to say that I don't care, or I'm not concerned of how others feel towards me. As a matter of fact, at times I can be hypersensitive and yes, even petty! Yet at the end of the day - after all is said and done - something inside drives me to be Mike McClure. I'm loud; there's nothing quiet about me. I'm an in your face, take me, or leave me kind of fellow

Why am I writing a book entitled *Life Out Loud?* The answer is for several reasons, which again will be revealed as you journey through the pages of this book, but mostly because I have learned a lot on this road called life and I want to share it with you.

I will lend this clue, though. Each chapter reveals an area in our lives, that until discovered screams for attention and absolute acceptance.

I guess I've written a book just to encourage everyone who reads it to make your life an investment that pays dividends in the lives of others, several years to come. In order to do so, we must all LIVE, LEARN, LOVE, LEAD, LAUGH and LEND OUT LOUD!!!!

CHAPTER ONE

LIVE OUT LOUD

We all come into this world kicking and screaming; putting forth all the effort we can to get attention. Everyone who is already living thinks it's a problem and wants to keep things quiet. But if you have any children of your own, then you know that they love to make noise.

If being heard has been our natural disposition since birth, I wonder why we get so offended and upset by the voices of others? The entire purpose of having a voice is for it to be heard. So often we try to quiet and stifle even our own voices and in essence, place a filter on who we are as people.

This reminds me of the times in my life when I was lost in a maze of discovery, walking in anonymity, and climbing the nob hills of nobody, searching for who I was and what I was supposed to be doing. I remember not being satisfied. I didn't use my voice in a way that projected confidence, surety, or self-awareness. This is because someone who doesn't know who they are, cannot use their voice as an adequate expression of self-identity.

God created us to be far more than we often recognize, and has more to say through us than we are often willing to communicate. Being unaware of who we are will either cause us to live a life that goes unnoticed or noticed for all the wrong reasons.

Trust me I get it. There was God, and then there was me. And I didn't know how to connect the dots between the two in order to bring the full picture of who I was to life.

God was standing on the back porch of nowhere, looking into the abyss of nothing, and calling everything into existence. Since the day God called the world into creation, it has remained the creation that He called it to be. God told Adam whatever he called the animals would be their name, and since then, nothing has ever changed.

Here I was, a living, speaking spirit in the earth, filled with the same creative power as God and unaware of my own potential. My identity, intimacy, and integrity in God were in jeopardy because I was lost and didn't have the courage to be who I was.

It wasn't until Father's Day in June of 1984 while serving my country in Europe that my life changed. I was sitting in a small military chapel filled with the most amazingly loving people I had ever met in my life. The preacher's wife had just delivered the most inspiring sermon on family, manhood, and an assortment of other subjects that all captured my attention, arrested my faculties, and in a nutshell, freed me to focus on what's important – Life and Living it to the fullest!!! In my own words "Living Out Loud!!!"

It was only when I relinquished everyone else's opinion, attitude, disposition, and philosophy of life as a source of significance, that I was able to come to myself. I mean my real, true self. When I met the real me, I realized I had been cheated of the longest lasting relationship I could ever have. I met a man named Jesus who genuinely loved me and met a version of myself that had been waiting to come alive. Someone touched me on the shoulder and said, "How are you doing Mike McClure. I'm Mike McClure, nice to meet you!" I had finally discovered me, the authentic me.

When I realized I was the crowning joy of all of God's creations, that I was the apple of His eye, it hit me like a sucker punch to the gut. I am all that and a bag of chips. I'm badddddd baby. It was then I decided I was done cheating God and myself by being less than what God called me to be.

I want you to come to the same realization of your value and what you mean to God. Only then can you embrace all of who He created you to be. You will even begin to embrace the parts of yourself that others don't understand. When you discover who God is, you pull back the world's lens of expectation and begin to see what God has invested in you and what He wants to do through you. Then and only then can you unapologetically be yourself.

Take me for instance, admittedly I'm a LOUD person. I laugh loud, and when I learn something new, trust me, everyone will know about it. No one has ever referred to or described me as a quiet, timid, soft-spoken person. But once I got a whiff of who I was in Christ, all the demons in Hell weren't enough to keep me quiet.

JESUS said in the book of John 10:10, that HIS very purpose and reason for coming into this World is to make us aware of the GOD-kind of life that's available for everyone who's bold enough and bad enough to accept it.

Listen to how Jesus speaks from this passage: "The thief comes only in order to steal and kill and destroy. I came that they may have and enjoy life, and have it in abundance [to the full, till it overflows]." AMP

Do you notice the word overflow? Overflow!!!

Usually, when something is overflowing, it is done by accident, like when you fill a cup too full of juice or run too much water in the bathtub. And then you must try and clean up your mess. So, you're telling me that God sent Jesus so that He could intentionally create overflow in my life? So that His goodness could spill out from the inside of me into every area of my life and even spill over into yours on purpose? That's enough to make a person shout!

My constitution for life is founded and rooted in these writings that convinced me that JESUS came to give Mike McClure life and that life more abundantly. More expressly put, in supernatural over abounding floods. The good news is this scripture wasn't just for me. This scripture is for anyone that would be brave enough to take hold of it and say with confidence, "THIS IS MINE."

Now tell me how and why this granted promise should be hidden or toned down? It shouldn't! And because of this truth, I can't help but live out loud. You may still be wondering; so what does it mean to Live Out Loud?

It is about more than the volume in your voice or being seen and heard just for the sake of getting attention.

To me, living out loud means I live my life in the open, no secrets, full throttle, all out for JESUS! I take full advantage of every opportunity to excel and do it unapologetically, wide open for the world to see. Remember Mike McClure told you this, "Life is your gift from GOD, what you make of it is your gift back to HIM."

We should make it our mission in life to live every day in such a degree that there's no possibility of regretting not having taken full advantage of each moment. Every opportunity we seize as our own creates the momentum that propels us into the purpose and destiny of God. If you have ever heard the saying, "There is never a dull moment," this should be true of all of us. Any moment that we are not taking captive as our own is being left up to chance. And why would we want to leave anything up to chance when God has given us the authority to take our moments captive and allow them to serve us in living our life out loud.

Merriam Webster defines life as the quality that distinguishes a vital and functional being from a dead body.

You're either living or you're dead. Some people are dead men and women walking and don't even know it. We can get so caught up in the rat race of life, that by the time we realize it is void of purpose and passion, we already have one foot in the grave. We think that the breath in our body is an indication of life, and though it may be the evidence of our existence on earth, it is no way a sign that we are truly living. Without the revelation of who we are, we are merely existing and turning the wheel of life just like I was, until God hit me on the head and said, "Hey, I called you for more than this."

I love what Charles R. Swindoll said about life, and I quote, "Life is 10% what happens to you and 90% how you react to it."

We could sit and talk about the hand we were dealt, the family we were born into, or the struggles we all have. And although I am sure all those points are valid, and in many ways, can turn into stumbling blocks. There is a time in everyone's life when we must decide for ourselves who we want to be.

If I were to spend my time dwelling on the consequences of the fallen state of this world, I would be doing you a disservice. I could instead be talking about the reward of living brightly and boldly in the abundant life afforded to us by Christ. Yeah, some bad things happened, now how are you going to react to it?

It's your turn now; the ball is in your court and no past hurt or mistake can hinder you unless you allow it to. Don't give up on your God given identity because of the hurts and pains of life. It is time for you to rise to the occasion and live out loud.

I too have been through my fair share of trials, but I tend to react out loud for the entire world to see, that I may in some little ways, help someone else better handle life's challenges and choices. If we go through difficult times without learning from them, then it was all in vain. Challenging times produces a voice within us that others may see as nothing more than noise.

What may be considered noise to some makes other people feel better about themselves. I can make noise around a sick person or someone struggling in life, and change the atmosphere. Not because I am something, but because the God in me is EVERYTHING.

I'm not doing this because I want to be somebody, but because I am exactly who God said I am. My life is not to be characterized by being small, insignificant, nothing, never being noticed by anybody, or not ever making a sound that echoes in time. We are to be a city on a hill whose light cannot be hid, a candle that men sit on top of a candlestick to light up the darkness. I didn't make this up; God said this about you and me.

"You are the light of the world. A town built on a hill cannot be hidden. Neither do people light a candle and put it under a bowel. Instead, they put it on its stand, and it give light to everyone in the house." – Matthew 5:14-15 NIV

Did you notice that the lit candle gives light to everyone in the house? There are people around you that you have been praying for, wishing someone would come their way and point them to Christ. But God is wanting you to take the shade off your own head so you can be the light that shines bright before those who are closest to you. Not only this, but in the chapter before God calls us salt. He says that we are the seasoning in the world. Have you ever had some chicken without seasoning? I don't know about you, but I would be throwing mine away.

And that is exactly how the Bible describes someone who is not walking in Christ's respected light. They aren't good for anything. When we don't take ownership of who we are, we become nothing more than a number, blending in with a world who is in desperate need of someone to step up and step out.

"You are the salt of the earth. But if the salt loses its saltiness, how can it be made salty again? It is no longer good for anything, except to be thrown out and trampled under foot." Matthew 5:13

If only you can be the seasoning, if only you can be you, what is the rest of the world going to do if you don't show up to add some spice and flavor? No one else can be you! Christ shines in you in a way that He can't do through anyone else. He wants the world to experience Him through you. But that can only happen when you are confident in who God is and who you are because of Him.

When we try to conform ourselves to the image of others, we are only dimming the light of Christ. God isn't going to ascribe to a fake version of you to touch others. He needs your background, your calling, your gifts, your culture, and your personality to reach people like you. So be you... proudly, and loudly.

No one can make you live out loud. It's a choice that you make for yourself. By choice, I want to live out loud, to live in the open. Yes, it comes with push back, yes, I have been told I am a showoff and show out, that I need to be quiet and have humility. But humility never meant being quiet and if that is a lie which has been keeping you silent, let me help to dispel it right now. Humility is about knowing who we are in Christ, it means acknowledging that I, Mike McClure, is nothing alone, but with God, I am just as Jesus is right now! (1 John 4:17)

I am as blessed as Jesus is, I am as healthy as Jesus is, I am at peace just as Jesus is right now. How in the world do you expect me to keep that under wraps? I mean, if you want to keep quiet about something so awesomely amazing, that's on you. But I couldn't keep this good news quiet even if I wanted to.

Jesus was as humble as they come but He didn't live His life under a rock, whispering whenever He had something to say. He stood on hills and boats, talking to the multitude without a microphone or a podium. He healed the sick, cast out demons, and turned over tables for the disrespect of the moneychangers in the temple. Now, that is the kind of humility I want to walk in. Jesus lived out loud without apology.

When Jesus saw things in the temple that displeased Him, He acted. Have you ever thought about the whip he made? You must be intentional to sit and braid a whip together. Jesus took time and willful thought in what He was doing. This wasn't some random act of rage. This was an example of a humble man who wasn't afraid to live His life, or His dissatisfaction of others' disregard for God out loud.

If there was anyone who got crazy looks at Him, had rumors about him, or had people disrespect Him for living out loud, it was Jesus.

Jesus was so radical about the things of God that He had no choice but to live out loud. It was as if He said, "My Father's house is not being portrayed in a way that would please Him." There was a force on the inside of Him, that would not allow Him to sit back and be content with suppressing His identity and purpose.

What things in your life need a good whipping? We all have areas that require our intentional effort in order to make necessary changes so that we too can live out loud, and unashamed as Jesus did.

Speaking of shame, do you remember Adam and Eve and how they lived in the garden? The Bible says that they were naked and unashamed. They were so in tune with God and who they were, that their nakedness was not seen as anything to feel ashamed of. But once they ate of the tree of the knowledge of good and evil, they then felt ashamed of their lack of clothing.

This is still happening with us today. When we tap into the mind of Christ concerning us, we become unashamed of who we were created to be. But just like Adam and Eve, when we eat from the tree of negativity that the world offers, we begin to hide who we are.

My goal, my aim, and my purpose in life and in writing this book is to give people liberty to understand and to know that it's alright to be out front in who you are in Christ. It's okay to walk into your Clark Kent phone booth and walk out into your superman life. It's okay to boldly reflect the new creation that you are in Christ.

There's a part of us that has always cried out for attention. Even since the days of our childhood. We can see it more in this age of social media than any other time. Everyone is sitting behind their phones, with their posts, their filters, and their ring lights yelling "look at me." I understand the desire, possibly more than most.

Something has always driven me to be noticed. God has put something inside of me to be seen and heard. Not because I am something to look at but because God has things that He has done in my life that He wants others to see. And it's not because I have the perfect words to speak, but because there is a testimony in my mouth that only I can convey.

If it's wrong to desire to be seen, then why are pastors on pulpits? If it's wrong for us to speak out loud and be heard, then why do singers have microphones. Why is the spotlight put on the talented and the gifted for the entire world to see? It is because the gift is not to be stored and hidden away. Every talent we are given by God should be given back to Him with interest. I don't know about you, but this is my life and I enjoy doing what God has anointed me to do.

When I think about the psalmist who wrote "you were fearfully and wonderfully made" (Psalm 139:14), it makes me ponder why God would store all that awesome fear and wonderment in us just for us to then hide it in a quiet re-served life that no one ever takes notice of? He didn't, and if we could get past our fear of other's opinions and our past mistakes, we could all live out loud. What is there to be afraid of?

Living out loud with wisdom

In my opinion, the only danger to living out loud is living a life out loud that is not worth immolating. Shining light on a life that you are afraid to see is a danger. You are allowing others to judge you in a season of life that wasn't meant for others to see.

Although I do wholeheartedly believe that we were all meant to live out loud, I also believe there are times and seasons where we must focus on our personal growth privately, and we need to know the difference.

There is a reason why Moses spent time in the wilderness before God used Him; there is reason why Saul spent time in the wilderness before Paul could come on the scene. When we embrace our wilderness season as the transformation process that it is, we will make a grand exit like a butterfly coming out of its cocoon.

Living out loud doesn't mean making yourself vulnerable to the point of self-sabotage and demise. It is wise to seek God on what parts of your life can be shared publicly and what parts still need to be kept tucked away and whom they need to be tucked away from.

We only do damage to ourselves when we live a life out loud that no one else can gain from or find value in. Living a life out loud that does not honor you or God is a detriment to yourself. Living a life that does not make your spouse proud to be your spouse and your children honored to be your children, or living a life in the open that no one needs to see is a danger to you and those who are influenced by your actions.

We want to thrive in a life that causes heaven to rejoice. Living a life that causes a smile to come upon the face of your savior is one that should be lived out loud. I say to you today, pump up the volume! Live your life to the fullest, be all you can be, stand tall, speak from the mountain.

Live every moment and every second of your life out loud in and for Christ with wisdom.

Who do they say I am?

One day when Jesus was walking with His disciples, He asked, "Who do men say that I am?" There were some good answers but those aren't important now. The lesson that was most important to me is that Jesus can only be to us who we perceive Him to be. If we don't recognize God as healer and provider, then He isn't able to manifest himself fully in those areas.

In what way do the people you care about perceive you? Jesus didn't ask just anyone this question. He asked the people who He spent the most time with; those who were dearest and closest to Him.

Ask your friends "Who do you say I am?" And when you ask this; what you are really asking is, what have I said, what have I done, who have I been, who will I become, what will be my legacy when I'm done?

What deposit have we made in the life of others that they should remember us? Was anyone's life positively impacted due to your living out loud? Can anyone say they are better because they met you?

My dream is to build a better me now so I can help someone else be a better them tomorrow. I do that by not hiding - by putting all of me on display. I pour everything that God deposited in me out, so that others can taste and see that the Lord is good through His work in my life.

Living out loud is all about magnifying Jesus, so that we can shine the light back on Him in all we do.

When we magnify God, he will magnify us. According to the word, we will have favor with both God and men when we embrace His mercy and walk in His truth (Proverbs 3:3-4).

It is easy to get caught up in this life with living for others, which is why we must be sure that we are living out loud for the right reasons. And the only reason should be God.

"But let the one who boasts boast about this: that they have the understanding to know me, that I am the Lord, who exercises kindness, justice and righteousness on earth, for in these I delight, declares the Lord." – Jeremiah 9:24

What else could we possibly have to boast about? I have made many accomplishments (as I am sure we all have), but when I look back, I know that God was behind them all. I remember who I was before I ran into Jesus, and He wasn't anyone who was worth calling home about. But Mike McClure after Jesus is a man to get to know. Because I know whenever anyone encounters me, they encounter the God in me, Jesus Christ himself, and that is something to live out loud about.

Live Your Struggles Out Loud.

Although we must be wise about the parts of our life that we share with the world, it is good to have someone in your corner who you can live even the most secret parts of your life out loud with. One of the biggest mistakes that we can make in our attainment of independence and self-proclaimed success is to deny our need for God and other people.

As much as we would like to think the phrase, "I don't need anybody" is true, it couldn't be any more untrue. We need people to give us insight from a perspective that we may not be able to see from. We need someone in our life who can give us an outlook that we may not have seen before or to just be a listening ear when life feels overwhelming, and we just want to be heard in a safe space. The Bible can't stress the importance of wise counsel enough.

"The way of a fool is right in his own eyes, but a wise man listens to advice." - Proverbs 12:15

"Where there is no guidance, people fall, but in an abundance of counselors, there is safety." - Proverbs 11:14

"Listen to advice and accept instructions, that you may gain wisdom in the future. Many are the plans in the mind of a man, but it is in the purpose of the Lord that they will stand." Proverbs 19:20-21

Just read through the book of proverbs and you will discover the importance of having sound advice. When we hide our struggles, all we do is empower them. One of the most important parts of living out loud is living your life out loud before God. He already knows your mess, because there are no hidden skeletons in the closet between you and Jesus.

We can't live life fully in front of others if we don't live it openly before God. Our vulnerability and surrender in our private time with God open the door for healing, restoration, strength, and deliverance. It is our willingness to live out loud before the Lord that empowers us and creates the inward transformation to live out loud before others.

We often do the opposite when met with guilt and shame by our life choices. We hide our faces from God thinking that He is like men and will judge us for our faults. But God wants us to turn to Him in these times more than ever because these are the times that we need Him most. The world will write you off, but God will empower you and cause you to live even louder than before.

I encourage you to live your life with transparency and vulnerability before God, unhidden and exposed for the scalpel of God to come in and remove what doesn't belong, then heal what is broken and give what is needed.

Live your victory out loud.

Living out loud is valuing every experience in your life, because God is using them all to bring forth good. Every valley is designed to be a lesson that will help us to live louder, greater, and better than before. If you remember, Jesus was baptized by John the Baptist and affirmed by His Father in heaven while the Holy Spirit descended on Him like a dove.

But the very next episode of His life, that very same Spirit led him to the wilderness to be tempted.

"And when Jesus was baptized, he went up at once out of the water; and behold, the heavens were opened, and he [John] saw the Spirit of God descending like dove and alighting on Him. And behold, a voice from heaven said, this is my Son, Mu Beloved, in Whim I delight! Then Jesus was led (guided) by the [Holy] Spirit into the wilderness (desert) to be tempted (tested and tried) by the devil." – Matthew 3:16-17, 4:1

This encounter with Satan was recorded because Jesus experienced life out loud. He used those moments to help other people, teach His disciples, and to guide us today. Jesus didn't hide anything in His life. He showed us how we ought to walk in every area of life, whether it be temptation, sadness, or joy. Jesus lived out loud for our example and He is still living life out loud through us as an example to the world.

I want to talk to those who have dealt with debt, bad credit, divorce, or falling out with children. I want to say to you; do it out loud. What do I mean by that? Learn from it and teach others what mistakes not to make. Its grievous for the moment, but afterwards, it is going to work in you the peaceable fruits of righteousness. Don't keep your past struggles to yourself. You didn't go through the hard knocks of life, just for yourself. Of course, you learned your own lessons along the way, but it is also so you can teach others and prevent them from going through the same path.

The only way that you can live your past mistakes out loud is to stop seeing yourself as a victim. A victim mentality will keep you quiet and subjected to the ideas that you are less than the high price that Jesus paid for you. But when you see your past and your mess-ups from a stance of victory, all you see are testimonies. You do know what the Bible says about testimonies, don't you?

"And they overcame him by the blood of the lamb, and by the word of their testimony." - Revelation 12:11 NIV

As long as you keep Jesus in His rightful place in your life, there isn't one circumstance, trial, or tribulation, that shouldn't be seen as a victorious testimony on the other side. If you wrestled with sexuality, don't keep your story in the dark. The very thing that nearly took you out is going to be what keeps someone else out. The very thing that almost killed you is going to keep someone else from dying. The very poverty that you finally walked out of is going to keep someone else from settling for the broke life. Live your victory out loud for someone else to step into.

Stop keeping your life a secret; others need help, others need to know.

Change the Family Dynamic

What is so amazing and powerful about living out loud is getting to set the example for other men and women. As a father and husband, having a family is one of the greatest joys of my life. I am proud to say I have been married to Angela almost forty years and been with her since 13 or 14 years old (and for those trying to do the math on how old I am, mind your business).

During those many years of marriage, we have both learned valuable lessons, we have both grown and matured in many ways. But what good would any of that have been if we were not able to allow our children to witness any of it so that they can gain insight and wisdom for their own lives.

It is vital that women as wives and mothers, daughters and friends, learn to live their life out loud. Your family and friends need your guidance, your intuition, and your outlook on life in general. Never look down on who you are as a woman, as a mother, or as a wife. You have been supernaturally gifted with a role and divine placement, and what you have on the inside of you deserves to be lived out loud. The next generation of women need to hear how you got through and what you did when times were difficult.

As men, we also have a duty to live our lives out loud for our families. The word husband literally means by definition, 'he who decides.' As a husband and a father, I choose to live my life out loud for my family. When I make myself transparent and vulnerable in front of my children, I am answering questions that they may never have the courage to actually ask. I am helping them decide what type of great men and great women they are going to be.

I don't hide my struggles from them, so that they can have confidence in what they can handle when they struggle. I allowed my kids to see me from the proper perspective, I allowed them to see me tired and stressed out, but I also made sure they saw the way I handled those situations. Our families need to see the good, the bad, and the ugly. We hide things from them thinking that it is for their own protection, when it is really a result of our own shame, insecurity, and fear of failure.

Instead of turning on the television, I opened up my heart and turned on the channel of life and allowed them to view me. I gave them the chance to view me as I truly am. Not just as Mike McClure the father, but as Mike McClure the husband, the man, the friend, the pastor, the teacher, and the student.

Many of my children's life lessons were not choreographed, planned out, or well-studied. The best lessons came as real-life experiences that I had the courage to live out loud in front of them. I believe families will be stronger, marriages will be healthier, and children will have the desire to be greater when we can live authentic lives before them.

In the words of my spiritual son, when the Bible says we were all created in the image of God, that word means we were all created to be icons. When you put this book down, I'm praying that something causes you to periodically pick it up in order to be inspired again, to live out loud, to be an example, and to be a driving force in the world to cause men, boys, and girls to be everything that we are called to be.

LEARN OUT LOUD

Proverbs 4:7 declares, "In all your getting. get under-standing."

U nderstanding in the Greek means to "entertain." So, in all your getting, get entertained, and have the ability to entertain. We retain what entertains us and block what bores us. Entertain means to arrest and hold one's attention.

The writing of Hosea really inspires me – No; it is more like a charge; filling me with hunger and thirst to learn all I can about anything and everything there is, especially about my God and myself.

"My people are destroyed for lack of knowledge: because thou hast rejected knowledge, I will also reject thee, that thou shalt be no priest to me..." (Hosea 4:6).

I learned that the word "priest" literally means "bridge". A bridge is a structure built to span a physical obstacle, such as a body of water, valley, or road, without closing the way underneath. It is constructed for the purpose of providing passage over the obstacle, usually something that can be detrimental to cross otherwise. God is literally saying that we cannot serve as a "bridge" for His people if we lack knowledge. When we reject knowledge, we don't have the solid construction to carry the weight of God's people and will do more harm than good.

I realized that if I'm to be the bridge that others use to cross over, I must know as much as possible, because how can I assist those in need if I don't even understand their plight? In fact, God Himself, had to contend with the same issue. How could He judge humanity unless He had first-hand knowledge of their challenges and victories, fears and sorrows, pains, and fleshly desires? To get this knowledge, He came down and lived among men in the form of His only begotten son, Jesus.

Jesus experienced every temptation known to man. He had to understand the psychological and biological phenomenon that causes mankind to think and act the way they do. Learning Out Loud is an intentional approach to learning. It means learning to develop yourself holistically: mind, body, and spirit. We are triune beings, and every part of our beings must be developed and strengthened.

I seek to learn or be "entertained" by every experience I encounter in life. I love asking questions and discovering the endless possibilities of their answers. I'm never silent about the things I desire to know, and I'm never too embarrassed to admit what I do not know. Instead, I challenge myself to never be caught not knowing that thing again.

I really believe knowledge is power, but let's delve a little deeper into what this cliché really means.

Knowledge Is Power?

How is knowledge power? Is the mere fact that you have heard and remembered a fact a point of power? I contend that knowledge is not really power as there are many people who have a great deal of knowledge and yet have no power. People have knowledge of what is right and what is wrong but lack power to control themselves. People have knowledge that smoking causes cancer but don't have the power to quit. We know that too much salt and sugar causes health issues, but still don't have the power to resist pork chops, fried chicken, macaroni and cheese, sweet potato pie and peach cobbler smothered with ice cream. So where is the power? The fact is, knowledge is not power. Instead, *Applied* knowledge is power.

The Book of James attests to this when speaking about the power of faith. In James 2:17, James writes, "...faith by itself, if it does not have works, is dead." Just as the power of faith is found in the working of faith, the power of knowledge is found in its execution. Knowledge without execution is nothing more than floating echoes in the void of a person's brain. They add no value to the life of the thinker or "knower" or the lives of others.

Learning Out Loud means executing and sharing your knowledge for the benefit of yourself and others. Notice I said for the benefit of others. No one likes a know-it-all who wants everyone to know how smart they think they are. I have found that most of those people have no more power than the power to irritate a crowd. They usually are jacks of many trades and masters of none. Learning out Loud is not a boastful lifestyle, it is a benevolent one. It doesn't seek its own glory.

Jesus is the absolute example of Learning Out Loud. He studied everyone around Him. As soon as He turned 12, He headed straight to the synagogue to learn. Here we had the Son of the true and Living God, going to the temple to study and learn – to teach and to be taught. Yet, Jesus, in all of His power and knowledge, performed many miracles and told the beneficiaries to "tell no one".

When the scribes and Pharisees brought the woman caught in adultery to Jesus, commanding Him to cast judgement upon her, He did not take the opportunity to battle wits and debate. He simply stooped down and started writing something in the ground. After they kept pushing Him, Jesus simply said, "He that is without sin among you, let him first cast a stone at her" (John 8:7). Jesus had knowledge of His adversaries and their true intent to tempt Him. He had knowledge of the woman caught in the act of adultery. He had knowledge of the law and did not debate it. Instead, He offered the man who was without sin to execute the law. Jesus utilized His knowledge to be a blessing— a "bridge"—of forgiveness.

Learning Out Loud is powerful in its simplicity. You don't have to be the loudest in the room to Learn Out Loud. You don't have to have the last word or have a voluminous vocabulary. You just need to speak truth to power. Sometimes one sentence, like the sentence Jesus spoke to the scribes and Pharisees, is enough to speak to every person in a crowded room individually. Jesus spoke 15 words and it touched every scribe and Pharisee in the crowd differently. It travelled into their minds and had a full conversation about each of their individual sins and brought conviction to their hearts. That's the power of Learning out Loud!

Learning the Power of the Mind

Learning is often confused with academics, but it is more than just getting intellectual knowledge or "book knowledge". Learning how to use your mind is the first step in Living Out Loud, because "as a man thinketh in his heart, so is he" (Proverbs 23:7). Your thoughts control your actions, and your actions control your outcomes. Confucius said, "The man (woman) who thinks he can and the man who thinks he can't, are both right."

In these two quotes, we realize that we can literally create our existence — the lives we love or the lives we hate — through the way we use our minds. A person who is perfectly healthy can think themselves into sickness. There are individuals who suffer ailments or diseases for which they have no symptoms, because in their minds, they are convinced that they are sick. There are also individuals who have had debilitating injuries, but they thought themselves to health.

The human brain is so powerful and yet we only use a fraction of its capacity. Perhaps, when Adam and Eve fell from grace and ate from the Tree of Knowledge of Good and Evil, humans lost the direct connection to the source that would allow us to tap into the full potential of the brain. Yet, we must utilize the strength that we have and learn to maximize it.

Learning is the seed for creation and the mind is the incubator. The more we learn, the more we can create. This immutable law can be used for or against us. If we learn good, we will create good. If we learn bad—no matter how badly we want good—we will create bad.

Imagine a set of exact twins are born and separated. One is taken to a home in the north, and one to a home in the south. The northern child is taught that he is strong, smart, and resourceful, and that he can accomplish any goal to which he sets his mind. The southern twin is taught he is weak, unintelligent, and clumsy, and that he will never have a prosperous life.

Now, imagine that both twins grow up and move to the big city where they can make millions of dollars and live the life of the rich and famous, or become poor and destitute. They both grew up to be the same height, size, and weight. They both look exactly alike. No one can tell the difference between the two. They are both able bodied and healthy. They both moved to the big city with $100 to their names. What kind of life do you imagine the northern twin will create, and what kind of life do you think the southern twin will create?

Look at a person's life and you will see the proof of what they think about day and night. Hebrews 11 stated that "faith is the...evidence of things not seen." A person's life is the "evidence" of their faith which is the "unseen thoughts." They are creating the reality they learned through life experiences, trials and errors, things they witnessed, and most importantly things they heard.

The Bible states "faith cometh by hearing." (Rom. 10:17). Godly faith cometh by "...hearing by the word of God", but we also grow faith in the negative and ungodly things we hear as well. Many people have been told that they are "no good" and they have grown to have faith in that lie. When good things start to happen, they become afraid and sabotage themselves because good things go against their faith in the "no good".

We are constantly learning something (good and bad) but Learning Out Loud requires that we take control of that knowledge and utilize it to our advantage and the advantage of the Kingdom. Proverbs 23:7 reads, as a man "thinketh in his *heart*..." This is significant because it implies that we don't have to accept every thought that we receive in our *heads!* Thoughts that come to our heads must be accepted in our hearts before they have the power to create our realities. Thus, we must learn to reject fleeting thoughts and hold only to the knowledge, wisdom, and truths of God.

This is not God's responsibility. It is your responsibility to control what you Learn and think in your heart. God has given you the house, but it is your responsibility to take care of it. When you hear negative words about you, your life, environment, or circumstance, you don't have to receive them as truth. In fact, the Bible speaks on multiple occasions about controlling your thoughts:

Philippians 4:8 tells us, "Finally, brethren, whatsoever things are true, whatsoever things are honest, whatsoever things are just, whatsoever things are pure, whatsoever things are lovely, whatsoever things are of good report; if there be any virtue, and if there be any praise, think on these things."

In all the scriptures concerning your thinking, none of them suggest that God will control your thinking for you. It is up to you to choose what you will believe and upon what you will meditate. It does not mean it will be easy to unlearn what life and others have taught you over the years, but with God's help, you can learn new paradigms and create new belief systems. But be warned, even after you have opened your mind to new beliefs, your old fleeting thoughts will return, but if you don't let the passing thoughts take that 18-inch dive into your heart, you can expel them like other wastes.

Learning Is the Seed of Creation

Now that we understand how Learning Out Loud empowers us, let's discuss the kind of power we are given. We're going around a sharp curve, so hold on tight.

When God created man, "in the likeness of God made he him; male and female created he them..." (Gen. 5:2). What does that mean? Does that mean that God has a human face, 10 fingers, 10 toes, two legs, two kidneys, a liver, or genitalia? How could that be if God is a spirit? Clearly, we are not created in God's *physical* image. Then what makes us like God? The thing that makes us like God is our ability to create. No other creature was created to think of invisible, non-existent things, and bring them to reality. Learning Out Loud is about using your unique mind and its unbridled power to create.

Ravens can create tools out of sticks, Octopus can camouflage their bodies to look like anything around them, and dolphins have the power of sonar—that would be cool for humans—but none of them can create architectural buildings, write works of art, paint masterpieces or compose songs that move angels. These powers to create are God-given and God says that His gifts are "without repentance" (Roman 11:29). Thus, we have this power to create good or bad.

This ability to create is not just a gift, it is a responsibility. Dare I go further, it is more than a responsibility, it is a command by which we will be held accountable. I'll give you some time to digest that. In fact, I need some time to digest that one... Okay, let's get back to it. When God created man and woman, He gave them marching orders. He told them to "be fruitful and multiply". When God said be fruitful, He was talking about man's internal integrity. When God said "multiply," He was commanding man to create. Here, we see that God did not want man to create just anything, He was commanding man to create that which was of benefit to mankind, the world, and the kingdom of God.

How serious is God about this command to Create? I'll give two examples of how serious God is about His expectation that we create. The first example I'll use is Jesus and the fig tree. We all know the story, and if you don't, here you go. In Matthew 21:19, we find that Jesus is walking with His disciples, most likely after a long day of ministering. Jesus was hungry and saw "a fig tree in the way." Jesus' tongue must have started watering, because He clearly really wanted a fig. When He got to the tree and found no *fruit*, He declared "Let no fruit grow on thee henceforward forever."

Jesus cursed the tree forever because it was not producing. I've always wondered; was Jesus personally offended by the fact that the tree did not produce fruit for the Son of God? Regardless, whether the tree was in season or not, Jesus expected it to "be fruitful and multiply" and when it did not, it was cursed and "withered away." If a fig tree can get that response for not bearing figs, how much more does God expect humanity to create what He has put within us?

The second example is the Parable of the Talents (Matthew 25). In this parable, a rich man gives three of his servants some cash to invest while he went away on a trip. The Bible uses the word "talents" which serves a double meaning as God has given us all talents that we must use for His glory but in this story, the talents represented money. The first servant was given five talents. The second servant was given two, and the third was given one.

The first servant "traded" with his talents and doubled his investment. He turned his five talents into ten. The second servant also invested his two talents and doubled his money, turning two into four. The third servant, however, was afraid that he would lose his talent and so he hid the money in the ground thinking he would please the master just by returning what he was given. When the master returned, he was excited to find out how his servants increased his money. The first servant reported, "here, I have made you five talents more. (v.20)" The master was ecstatic. "Well done, good and faithful servant. You have been faithful over a little; I will set you over much. Enter into the joy of your master (v.21)."

The same happened for the second servant who was able to report the doubling of his two talents. However, when the third servant brought forward the same one talent that he was given, the master was extremely upset. "You wicked and slothful servant (v.26)" he rebuked. He told him that even if he was afraid to lose his money in trading, he could have at least given the money to the bank and let it earn interest.

The master took the one talent from the third servant and gave it to the first servant, then he "cast the worthless servant into the outer darkness. In that place there will be weeping and gnashing of teeth." Wow!! That seems rather harsh of a punishment, doesn't it? This and the fig tree parable seem like over reactions for what seemed like minor events. But when God commanded man to be fruitful and multiply, it was not "best wishes" parting words. It was a serious command which has kingdom significance.

We are always moving in one direction or the other. If we are not moving forward, we are moving backwards. The treadmill of life is always moving and if you stop walking you will be thrown off the back. We may think that we are safe in our comfort zones and that things are calm, but in actuality, we are moving backwards the longer we sit in complacence and are not creating. We are moving backwards and farther away from God's will. This leads to the neglect of those who need what God has put within us, hindering the work of God and opening the door for the enemy.

It's not a game. It seems like choosing comfort and complacency is not a big deal, but it is a dereliction of your spiritual duty worthy of a court martial.

Use Your Words

Learning Out Loud is most evident in the way you use your words. Words are containers. They carry life, death, and healing. If your words only stay in your head, they won't have any effect, but when they are released out of your mouth, the words will frame your world. Words are so important that God identifies Himself as "the Word." The Bible reads in John 1:1; "In the beginning was the Word, and the Word was with God and the Word *was* God"

God had to speak the words in order to create. Throughout the first chapter of Genesis, we can see that everything was brought into existence because "God said." The word of God was a force that brought something forth from nothing. If God had not opened His mouth to speak the words, nothing would have happened. The original seed was the Word of God.

This is why changing the way we think is not enough and why learning alone will not foster change and creation. We need to speak out of our mouths what we expect to see happen in our lives, what we desire of our business, and what we expect to happen. When our mouth starts moving, our life starts changing.

The same power that God has to speak and create is the same one that we can wield to bring our life into alignment with God's plans for us. When you learn, you use the power of your words to project that creative power into the atmosphere. Therefore, it is important to share what you learn. Jesus said it this way, "Go into all the world and preach the gospel [speak what you have learned] to every creature." Do you understand how powerful your words are? Do you understand that the Devil has no voice in this world save what we give him through *our* words?

The enemy has always been after our words. In the garden of Eden when Eve was tempted by Satan, she added to what God said in His commandment about the tree of knowledge of good and evil. You see; if the devil can get us to say the wrong thing, he can get us to taste of a life that was never intended for us to live.

What God said: But of the tree of knowledge of good and evil, thou shalt not eat of it: for in the day that you eatest thereof, thou shalt surely die.

*What Eve said: But of the fruit of the tree, which is in the midst of the garden, God hath said, Ye shall not eat of it, **neither shall you touch it, lest you die**.*

Eve did not have a clear understanding of the consequences that were set forth by God and it was also clear to the enemy once it was spoken out of her mouth. Those very words led her into making the worst decision of all mankind. This is why we must learn out loud and speak what is in our renewed mind into existence.

Our words are eternal. They never stop travelling or creating. This is why Isaiah wrote, "so shall my word be that *goeth* forth out of my mouth: it shall not *return* unto me void, but it shall accomplish that which I please."

When God speaks, His word travels until it is accomplished. When we speak, our words travel, and travel, and travel, until they find someone to accomplish them.

Have you ever verbally expressed an idea that you had in your mind? It may have been an invention or a business idea. After speaking your idea, you shrugged it off and never took any action, but later were surprised to see an infomercial of *your* exact product! Do you think that was a coincidence? I don't. I believe that when we speak words, we are planting seeds of creation. If you don't act on that seed, it will continue to grow until a receptive mind receives it and acts upon it.

Imagine if you could literally see your words travelling. Imagine being able to see the vibration bouncing from person to person, seeking to be picked up by the minds and spirits of other people. This is what is happening. Your words are always travelling and coming back to you, and they will not return void. When you speak negativity over your life, it keeps travelling, looking for someone or something to fulfill its mission.

We are careless and reckless with our words, as we believe they have died in the air simply because we can't hear them anymore. To the contrary, those words are travelling with purpose. Carelessly using our tongue is like carelessly using a loaded gun. Once shot, that bullet will do what it was designed to do — destroy anything in its path.

Imagine being put into an echo chamber for one full year where every word you speak bounces back and forth, like a ricocheting bullet. What words would you speak? What words would you want ricocheting around your mind?

Would you want to spend a year with the echoes of: "I'm stupid!" "Why can't I ever do anything right?" "I hate my nose?" Would you gossip and speak vicious and spiteful words? Or would you find soft, pleasant, melodious, and creative words that soothe your mind and heart? Imagine all of the words God hears being carelessly shot around the world. I know you have heard it before that when you know better, you do better; but when you know better, you actually speak better. Knowledge truly is power when we allow our words to be a product of our learning out loud, then our possibilities and potential are endless.

If Learning is the seed of creation and being "loud" or using your words is the release of that seed, then learning out Loud is a mandated process of creation. The biggest fool in the world is the man who rejects knowledge. He who cannot learn cannot be taught and thus he cannot create. If he can't create, then he can't walk in purpose.

The Obstacles of Learning Out Loud

We've talked about the importance of Learning Out Loud, the power and impact it has, and the reason we should Learn Out Loud. So, the question is, what is stopping us from doing it? In my opinion, there are three major obstacles that keep us from Learning Out Loud:

1. A fear of being wrong
2. Relationships
3. The challenge of change

Fear of Being Wrong

Why are we so afraid to be wrong? Have you ever been in a classroom and had a teacher ask a question for which you clearly knew the answer, but for some reason, your throat locked up when it was time to share the answer? You knew the answer as clearly as you knew your own name, but you waited—even if for a brief second—to see if someone else would answer.

Why do we hesitate? It isn't because we don't know the answer. It's because we are afraid of being wrong. We were afraid of looking stupid in front of our classmates. Afraid that we would make a fool of ourselves for being so eager to show how smart we were just to be completely wrong.

This fear of being wrong has stopped many of us from living the life we truly want and deserve. The fear of being wrong is really the fear of failure. However, as Christians, we must understand that we never fail, if we are following the direction of the Lord. There is never failure in God, but as Genesis 8:22 tells us, "As long as the earth remaineth, seedtime and harvest... shall not cease." In other words, every experience we have is a seed sown waiting for manifestation.

Failure is the seed of success. Some of us will plant many of those seeds that must take root first, and before it takes root, it must die. 1 Corinthian 15:36 explains "what you sow is not made alive unless it dies" (NKJV). There is no failure in Christ. What you sow must go through the germination period. Delay does not mean denial. Walk boldly in your anointing and the knowledge of God in your life.

Relationships

There's an old saying: "Show me your friends and I'll show you your future." Relationships have an indelible impact on your faith and the execution of your faith. 1 Corinthians 15:33 states "be not deceived, evil communications corrupt good manners." The people with whom we share our time, dreams, fears, and ambition, have the power to make or break us.

The worst enemy you can have is a bad friend. We know that our enemies seek our demise. We know not to believe their lies, and we know not to trust their honest intent to harm us. However, our friends have our trust and confidence.

Our friends and family are, many times, the most discouraging forces in our lives. Let's think about a few examples in the Bible where relationships attempted to interfere with God's people. When God and Satan made their wager that Job would curse God if His hedge of protection was removed, it was Job's wife who said "doest thou still retain thine integrity? Curse God, and die" (Job 2:9).

Think of that. She was the literal voice of Satan—verbatim! Satan's challenge to God was that Job would "curse God", and the woman closest to Job was telling him to "curse God and die" just as Satan wanted.

The next relationship was between Peter and Jesus. Peter was dear to Jesus. He was the one disciple who had the spiritual revelation of who Jesus truly was. When Jesus asked the disciples, "Who do people say I am?" the disciples ran down a list of public opinion, but Peter knew exactly who Jesus was. "Thou art the Christ, the son of the living God." Yet, even understanding who Jesus was, he still attempted to lead Jesus away from His appointed path.

After Jesus explained his purpose and how he would have to go to Jerusalem to be killed, Peter "rebuked" Jesus, telling him "Be it far from thee, Lord. This thing shall not be unto thee." Was Peter's intention to subvert the will of God? Of course not. He had good intentions. He wanted to protect a man he loved. Those who love us don't intentionally want to distract us from our goals, our purpose, or our mission in life; they truly want to protect us or save us from hardship. Job's wife was not a spiteful woman looking to cash in on Job insurance policy. She saw her husband suffering and wanted him to be spared the pain and heartache.

But what friends and family, and even we ourselves, fail to understand is that we can never grow to our fullest potential without burying the seed of our potential in the soil of hardship and struggle. There is one relationship that trumps all others and one voice that does the same; and that is the relationship and voice of God. We must not allow fleshly relationships to stunt our lives and our ability to Learn out loud. We must be bold enough to walk the path God has for us even if our closest relationships disagree.

The Challenge of Change

Learning out Loud is often hampered by our own fear of change. Have you ever been honest enough with yourself to admit that you are afraid of change? The reason that change is so fearful is because it makes you so uncomfortable. The power of learning out loud is that the more you learn, the more you will be changed.

Whether you want to change or not, new knowledge changes who you are. If you choose to utilize your knowledge, you have become a new man or woman. If you choose to ignore or avoid your knowledge, you have become a more disingenuous person who has chosen to avoid truth in order to maintain your status quo.

Now, let's be clear. When we discuss learning and knowledge, we're not referring to a passive gathering of information. For example: have you ever considered the words you have in your lexicon for which you do not know the actual definition? You've heard and used the words all of your life. Your parents, teachers and friends used the words, and so you too used the words. You even understand the context of the word and you use it correctly, but have you taken the time to actually learn the true meaning of the word?

Learning out Loud is about digging deeper than what we think we know and looking for the absolute understanding. It is this level of learning and knowledge that changes us. You cannot reverse what you have learned, and thus, you can never be the same. Some of us understand this truth and they run from knowledge and embrace the notion that "ignorance is bliss." The put their heads in the sand like the ostrich.

Peter's response to Jesus was an example of this. He received the pure and unadulterated truth from Jesus about the path ahead. However, Peter wanted everything to remain the same. He thought he, Jesus, and the other disciples would grow old together, build churches around town, and enjoy the miraculous adventures they had been experiencing over the previous three years. He didn't want that to change. And the fact is, if it would have been in his power, he would have stopped anything from changing his dream.

Guess what. A lot of us are making the decision to ignore and/or muffle the knowledge we have learned in an attempt to stop change. We like our comfortable lives. Even those who are uncomfortable would prefer their current discomfort because it is a discomfort they know. But if you're going to experience the fullness of your existence, you must embrace the challenge of change.

CHAPTER THREE
LOVE OUT LOUD

There is no louder form of expressing love out loud than the act that Jesus performed on the Cross. The Bible states there is "no greater love"—no louder expression of love—than laying down your life for a friend. Loving out loud in this context should not be confused with emotional and romantic displays of affection. Far from it. Loving out Loud is not about touching and smooching. Instead, loving out loud is about sacrifice of oneself for the benefit of another.

Loving out loud is about forgiving the unforgivable and embracing the repugnant. This is what God did for us. Our sins are loud, but God's love is louder. Which is why the Bible says, "Where sin abounds, there His grace does much more abound" (Romans 5:20). His love drowns out our sins until the only thing He hears are the melodious songs of mercy and grace.

Love in Action

Christians must not love in secret but in the open, for the world to see. We must love so loud that even those who hate us will have to take notice. How do we love out loud? We must first understand the loving out loud is not about words, it is about action. Janet Jackson put it this way, "What have you done for me lately." I'm not talking about superficial actions, but actions of pure love and spirit.

When you see your brother or sister in need, it is not enough to say, "I'm praying for you." So often we use this cliché expression of concern in order to put a check in our empathy box and then forget to pray later. However, God requires more than a passive prayer. He wants us to act. This message is abundantly clear in the parable of The Good Samaritan.

Not only did Jesus denounce racial and cultural discrimination and bias, but He also explained that the Samaritan showed true love because he went beyond words and showed his concern through acts of love and compassion. He wrapped and bandaged the bruises of the injured man, he provided shelter, and insured the continued care, until the man was fully recuperated.

What good is a prayer to a man starving? Prayer doesn't fill his belly, food does. What good is a prayer for the naked or homeless? Loving out loud is an action of love, not the sound. In fact, Paul put it best, "If I have not love, I am become as sounding brass, or a tinkling cymbal."

Not only are we all talk and no show when we talk about love without action, but Paul took it to another level and said that we are just making noise.

Am I suggesting that if you don't take tangible action to assist the needy that you are not loving out loud? Yes! That's exactly what I'm suggesting. If you are not loving out loud, then you are not loving. Even more, that is what the

Bible is saying. In Matthew 7:21-22 and Matthew 25:31, Jesus explains a harrowing reality.

Jesus explains that not everyone who calls Him Lord will enter into the Kingdom of Heaven. Wait! What? Jesus even goes further to explain that some of these people who will be cast into utter damnation will even say, "have we not prophesied in thy name? and in thy name have cast out devils? And in thy name done many wonderful works?"

Let's stop and digest what we are reading. Jesus is telling us outright that even if we claim Him as Lord and are even able to prophesy in His name, cast out devils, and work miracles, there is still the possibility that we will not be able to enter the Kingdom of God.

To the protests of these "preachers, prophets, and miracle workers," Jesus will say, "I never knew you; depart from me…"

Wait! What?! How can Jesus proclaim to have never known a person who has prophesied in His name? What could be missing? If we read a little farther into the scripture, we find Jesus providing another telling explanation of what will happen on the Day of Judgement.

In Matthew 25:31, He explains that when He comes into His kingdom, all of the nations will be gathered before Him, and at that time, He is going to separate "the sheep from the goats."

To the sheep, He will say, "come, ye blessed of my Father, inherit the kingdom prepared for you…" but to the goats, He will say, "Depart from me, ye cursed, into ever-lasting fire, prepared for the devil and his angels."

Now this is where it gets interesting. Jesus explains the qualifications that determined who were sheep and goats, saying: "For I was hungered, and ye gave me meat. I was thirsty, and ye gave me drink: I was a stranger, and ye took me in: Naked and ye clothed me, I was sick and ye visited me: I was in prison, and ye came unto me."

This confuses the sheep and the goats. They have no recollection of visiting, feeding, or clothing Jesus. Reading further, the Bible says "When saw we thee a stranger, and took thee in? or naked, and clothed thee? Or when saw we thee sick, or in prison, and came unto thee?"

Jesus replies, "in as much as ye did it unto the least of these, ye did it unto me."

In this scripture, Jesus explains that those who Loved Out Loud—showed love through action—He considered sheep and worthy of inheriting the kingdom of God, but those who did not show love in action, were not counted worthy.

John the son of Zebedee wraps the bow around it all in 1 John 4:7-8, writing, "Beloved, let us love one another: for love is of God; and everyone that loveth is born of God, and **knoweth** God. He that loveth not, **knoweth** not God, for God is love."

So how is it that Jesus could tell the people "I never knew you" even after they have preached and done wonderful works in His name. Simple. If you are not loving out loud as Jesus explained to the sheep and the goats, then you are not loving, and He that loveth not, "knoweth not God."

Wow, now that is deep. But we already know this to be true. Just think about relationships. What man or woman is going to accept a proclamation of love without the corresponding actions to solidify the words? What if you were constantly being told by a significant other that they loved you, but they ignored you and never gave you what you need whether that be physical, psychological, emotional, or monetary. One of two things would eventually happen. You would finally come to the realization that their professions of love are only words without truth, or you will get tired of that type of "love" and leave.

We all know that love requires actions, we just sometimes look over it when it comes to the things of God. All love, for all individuals even in our relationship with God requires corresponding action.

Loving out loud means that we must understand what love is, or for a better term WHO love is. Love is God, and many of us express love as a watered-down version, based off our own treatment, riding on the thin line of love and hate. We have all seen this type of love and it can often be far louder than the type of love that God has called us to walk in because it is more popular and may even feel better in the moment.

Loving out loud God's way includes self-sacrifice. The idea alone is foreign to many, but self-sacrifice is the exact act of Christ's death on the Cross and the embodiment of His entire life and ministry on the earth. Well, that was Jesus...right? Yes, but this same type of self-sacrifice is also expected of us if we are going to love the right way. Yes, there is a right and wrong way to love, and there is enough hurt in the world to prove it.

One of the first things that the Bible tells us if we want to be disciples is that we must deny ourselves. The amplified version says it like this.

Then Jesus said to His disciples, if anyone desires to be My disciple, let him deny himself [disregard, lose sight of, and forget himself and his own interests] and take up his cross and follow me. – Matthew 16:24

Jesus is in essence saying, "forget about you." I know you may be thinking, this requirement is to be a disciple not to love someone. Well, in the famous love chapter in 1 Corinthians chapter 13, where love is defined, verse five says that love is not self-seeking. I know this sounds completely opposite of today's version of love, but when we love out loud God's way, it is not only never failing, it is eternal.

Being selfless doesn't mean never being pleased or disregarding things that you like or enjoy. It means that you put someone else first and in doing so, guess what? You still end up pleased and fulfilled because God will love you in the same way He is asking you to love others.

When we love out loud selflessly, we capture one's attention to express that no matter who you are or what you have done, I'm loving you. And that is the type of love that heals hearts, empower others, and introduces people to Christ.

Love Is Honest

We can't address what it means to love out loud like God without talking about honesty. There are many people who enjoy having yes men and women in their life. This means having people who will agree with what you do whether it is wrong or right, and that is not real love. True love, the kind of love that lives out loud, is honest to the core, even when it hurts, and even when it means telling someone something they don't want to hear.

The Bible tells us that open rebuke is greater than secret love (Proverbs 27:5). Real love is being more willing to confront a wrongdoing than to hide your feelings. This is what many don't understand about God, they see the do's and don'ts in the word of God or live a life a certain way and get convicted by their actions. When this happens, they push God away because they don't like the way it feels but that is what love feels like. We just don't recognize it as love.

Being able to love out loud means that you can tell the truth but also accept the truth. No matter how hard honesty may hurt, it can be received when coming from a place of love and sincerity. Love is truth, love is honesty, and love is vulnerability.

Love on Display

Regardless of the situation and what is going on in our lives, love should always be on display. Stop hiding your love. Whenever there is an expression of love, it lets the world know that God is alive and well. When hugs are given, smiles are shared, laughs are exchanged, needs are met, truth is embraced, it not only says that people still love, but that there is a God who loves.

Let's Love Out Loud.

Don't love out loud to be braggadocios. You're not doing this to receive glory or honor and if you are, stop it! This isn't about us; this is about God. How would men know that you serve God unless you love. So many times, we see love as a noun, but love should be a verb.

"Love Is What Love Does"

Loving out loud is best expressed in action. There are certain things in life that cannot be hidden: Love, Respect, and Honor.

What is the opposite of loving out loud—It is not loving at all. If you're not loving out loud, are you loving? Where would man be if Christ's death was a secret?

If you want to win a man, LOVE HIM. Even the Bible says that it is the love of God shown through His goodness that causes us to change our ways.

"Or do you despise the riches of His goodness, forbearance, and longsuffering, not knowing that the goodness of God leads you to repentance?" – Romans 2:

Love in such a way that makes a man say, "What manner of man is this?"

Love is not a sound; it is the picture we paint. A color can be loud. Did you remember the Easter suits your mother bought you? Yeah, the pastel ones with the powder blue lining. They were loud. But if you would have left it hanging up in the closet, no one would have gotten to witness your Easter fit, and if we don't love out loud, there are so many people who won't get to witness God's love for the world.

What might make a person not want to love out loud?

1. You have to Love yourself. Loving yourself is about identity and self-service. What we give flows out of what we already possess. Love must start with you, and then it can be extended to others.

2. You have to deny yourself. You cannot love out loud if your main concern is you. You must be self-less. You must be a tool to serve. Our life is to be the solution.

3. You have to be vulnerable. I learned this years ago. My greatest area of vulnerability is not in my money, my vocation, or occupation. It was in my trash can. If a person sifts through my trash, they can learn anything they want about me. I used to work for the FBI. We learned in the FBI to sift through the trash. Many cases were closed due to what was found in trash bins. It would be a shame to discover more about a person in their trash bin than how they love in life.

4. Erasing the invisible line that separates openness from transparency. Openness means that I will truthfully answer. But transparency means that you will live in such a way that you don't have to ask. Many people are so jaded that they find it hard to trust love. When we love out loud and are transparent, they don't have to wonder.

Although life can get hectic, we must also find time to steal away with God. It is not hard to find ourselves with our love meter on empty and this if often because we have not filled up our tanks by spending time with love himself, God. If we are feeding on the word of God, it keeps the flesh at bay. Consequently, the feelings of being used and taken advantage of is squelched.

How do you deal with the pain, and rejection of loving out loud? After every moment of being less, you must have a moment of "never the less." At the point of nevertheless, our divinity supersedes our humanity. It's important that we all reach the not my will but thy will.

What people don't understand about the way love works is that we love from God, and it is God who loves us in return. The less we expect from others, the less we are able to be impacted by their actions or lack thereof. We should love out loud from our relationship with God and He will show His love for us in many forms and shapes. Having others embrace that love is just the icing on the cake.

Wanting to love this way is not often natural to us. Which means we must reach beyond our own selves into the heart of God to live our lives this way. The only other power on earth that is as strong as the will of God is the Will of man. God will not fight against the will of man. As much as God wants love through you, He needs your cooperation to make it happen.

Are you willing to cooperate with God so that He can show out though your love? Are you bold enough to put yourself to the side and say this prayer? "Lord, show me how to love like you do. Help me to see others from your heart and your eyes."

What kind of world would we have if we all loved out loud? We would have an end of the world as we know it. That's heaven on earth. That's literally having every thought right, and every deed right. I believe that is what we are going to have in heaven - The full expression of what it means to love out loud.

Can loving out loud overshadow the hating out loud we see in this world? It must. We speak what we really believe. 1 Peter chapter 4, says that love covers a multitude of sins, so when we share our love with the world, we cover the hate and wrongdoing that exist within it and instead encourage others to seek out that same source of love, which is Christ.

Loving Ourselves So We Can Love Others

Due to a fear of being alone, we often find ourselves attempting to love someone to our own detriment. Is that possible? Absolutely. We must understand that there are people who can be loved closely and intimately while there are others that must be loved from a distance to protect our own heart and mental health. Both acts are showing love but with the understanding that the action towards others will vary depending on your own ability and capability.

There are times when loving out loud must choose peace over companionship. I have to love you enough to set you free. Loving someone could mean wanting to see them happy even if it means the end of what you have with them. We must love ourselves enough to protect our own wellbeing and place of peace. We must love others enough that we don't hold them back from the direction of life that God has purposed them to walk in. Many times, we are not better together, we are Bitter together. The quicker we understand this, the sooner we become free to love ourselves; because those who love themselves are the greatest lovers of others.

Self-love~ Loving yourself out loud. Every act of love that we show anyone else should reflect the love we carry inside. I can only connect you to what I carry within myself. If I don't have love within, I cannot share it with you.

How Do You Learn to Love Yourself?

1. Plug into the source – How else can we see what God loves about us. If God gave himself for me, then I have to be willing to give myself for myself.

2. Be willing to feel our pain but take responsibility for our feelings.

3. Growth is not automatic, it is intentional. We have to be intentional in loving myself.

4. Discover what led you to the state you are currently in. Remember when God took a walk in the garden. When God asked Adam where art thou, he meant where you are mentally, emotionally, and

spiritually. He wanted Adam to come into a greater state of self-awareness.

5. Accept Responsibility for myself. Until we are able to acknowledge the part that we play, we can never make the necessary changes.

6. Stop! And do better – Don't put it off until Monday or even tomorrow. Stop what you are doing right now and make a conscious decision to do better.

CHAPTER FOUR

LEAD OUT LOUD

Leaders don't just dictate, delegate, or designate. Genuine leaders have a mandate!! Mandate means to give an authoritative order or command.

Leadership is influencing others to act, which can either produce good or bad results depending on how you are leading and what the motive is behind it. Regardless of whether you would consider yourself to be a leader, we all have some level of influence and the ability to impact the behavior, choices, and mindsets of others. When we realize we are all leaders, we can take more accountability in our leadership and make sure we are leading out loud with purpose and passion.

The foundation of any good leader is their heart. Our heart is the why behind our motives, it is the reason that we do anything. Even those who do not feel qualified to be leaders are acting out of their heart and are impacting others through those words and actions.

"He cared for them with a true heart and led them with skillful hands." - Psalm 78:72

If we care for those God has called us to impact, then we will be serious about how we lead out loud. Most of us have at least been under a leader or manager who did not care. Although they were physically present, their heart wasn't in it. Those type of leaders are easy to spot. They have no real compassion for those they lead, nor any true interest in the growth and elevation of others. These types of leaders will often cause others to leave as a result of their poor leadership.

We at the base level should want to see those around us reach new heights in their lives and business choices. And as a friend, we do what we can to help push them in that direction and that is a heart of leadership. Wanting to see others succeed and doing what we can to progress the vision is the foundation of leadership.

Caring with a true heart is the first step but the second and another equally important step is leading with a skillful hand. This means that we have developed a sense of expertise in a certain aspect of life and can lead others in that same area. We can't lead someone in something we have never done, nor can we lead them to a place we have never been. What is your area of knowledge and understanding? You will find that we often naturally share our areas of experience with others, which is leading out loud at its core.

We all have something that we do well. Whether it is math and showing others how to improve, raising children and helping other new parents, or playing basketball and giving other tips on how to enhance their game. Whatever you are good at, that you know most about, or your greatest area of change, are all things that someone else will be eager to glean insight on. There is always an opportunity to lead and if we are leading out loud, we have the power and impact to change a life, a generation, and even the world.

But that is only when others are open to hear what you have to say.

Leaders Are Trusted

If people are not open to your expertise or receiving what you have to say about a matter you are knowledgeable in, the next question we need to ask ourselves is, are we trustworthy? What have we done to earn the trust of those we influence? Are we someone that people can trust for valuable and honest advice? Can they trust us as a source of accurate information, or can they trust our apologies when we miss the mark?

The more trust someone has in us, the more influence we have over them. Leading out loud is only possible if those you lead trust that you care. No one wants someone leading them who is only out for self-interest and deceitful motives. If you take a retrospective look at your life, you will see people you trust, the impact they have on your life, and how they influence you. To have the greatest influence, we must have the greatest level of trust.

I realized the importance of trust in leadership mostly in my role as a father. The more your children trust you, the more access you have to them and consequently the more influence you have in their decision-making process and guiding their journey through life. This is the same for anyone. When people trust you, they let down their guard;

they let you in; they are even willing to take on your ideas and beliefs instead of their own.

I noticed the power of leadership back when I was a kid on the playground. I realized I was a leader myself as early as kindergarten; I recognized I could influence others to do the silly and playful acts that I did. In the Collegeville projects of Birmingham Alabama directly around the corner from the Como store, I would gather my buddies to play and always be the one who ended up shouting instructions. I noticed my friends would always follow my directions and from that point on, I always had a desire and the ability to be out front and lead the pack.

When I got older, my parents signed me to go into the military at 16. I was in basic training when my drill sergeant saw the leadership in me and made me a platoon leader. There was something in me that would naturally take charge. I was only in the military for a year when considered for sergeant three. And another year later came my recommendation for E6 staff sergeant. They awarded me the highest-level award you can receive, the ACROM Army Accommodation Medal with two oak leaf clovers.

I always felt destined to lead others in such a way that it would help them discover their dreams, reach their goals, and ascend to heights and levels that they could not attain on their own. I always felt like there was something that came on when I was around people who would not allow me to fade into the background.

There was a constant force pushing me forward to lead out loud in front of others and for others. You may think it is because I am a pastor. No; we all have the call to lead out loud. When God told us to go into all the world and spread the gospel, leading out loud is exactly what he was telling us to do.

I always knew in my life I could be a key element, a north star, and a driving force in the life of others. I still know it now, and God also called you to be that same force of influence. It may not be the way I do it, or how I would say it. But there is a specific group of people who are waiting for you to lead out loud. It is a travesty to have an opportunity to influence others meaningfully and not put it to use. One of the very purposes of Jesus' existence was to influence His followers to attain a level of living that pleases God. Jesus knew the power of leadership and influence, and so should we.

"My sheep hear my voice, and I know them, and they follow me." -John 10:27 NIV

The multitude didn't follow Jesus because of what He had, but because of His "stuff". They followed Jesus because of His influence, and His ability to impact every life that He ever encountered. He led with love first and spoke with authority and truth. The resounding sound of truth echoed out to those who had ears to hear and changed their lives. The leadership of Christ as head of our lives gives us the courage, determination, and love, that is necessary to take on the challenges of life and lead others to do the same. Those who walk in truth will always draw truth seekers to them.

Leading out loud draws people through love, not mandatory, forceful obedience. When people recognize the heart of a leader and evidence of their life, they will say, "I want to go where he/she is going" or "I want to change my life, let me see if this person can help me do it." It is time to take the horse by the reins and ride it.

We have been allowing life to drag us along and quiet our position as leaders on the earth, when we have been called for such a time as this. There will be challenges, changes, and choices, but leading out loud is being willing to accept changes, make choices and confront challenges and doing it in such a way that others willingly place their trust in you to get them where they should be.

"Where there is no guidance, the people fall, but in the multitude of counselors, there is safety." Proverbs 11:14 NKJV

In life, we can see many of the same mistakes, the same bad choices being made, and the same obstacles and mindsets holding people back that we once had, but this doesn't have to be so. If more people would lead out loud, sharing their knowledge, mistakes, and wisdom, they could lead others away from those same paths, places and decisions. We are all called to lead to some capacity, and once you find your place of leadership within you, don't keep it quiet.

You may still think that you don't have what it takes to be a leader, or maybe you don't feel you have the calling or skill to lead. BUT YOU DO. The breath in your lungs and heartbeat in your chest means you do. Whether you are a leader of few or many, of children or adults, God called you to lead someone, and you will affect others whether you recognize your influence or not. Anyone can do this if you use the elements of leading.

There are five elements that every leader needs if they are going to lead out loud:

1. Inspiration - The ability to awaken life in others. This is the area of your life where you have experienced breakthroughs and can now empower others to experience it as well.

2. Identification- Causing others to discover their true selves and where we find our purpose.

3. Motivation- Causing others to aspire to lead and driving them to develop leadership principles.

4. Deliberation- Causing others to rethink their principles and practices. This is where we get our priorities straight and aid in developing healthy mindsets.

5. Manifestation- Helping others to achieve biblical faith results. Manifestation is the proof that leading out loud is effective.

If we are going to lead out loud, we cannot afford to be bashful or shy, and we can't be afraid to take risks. Put me in a room full of people and I am going to rise to the top and find myself leading. Not because I am the most educated in the room or the most charismatic, but because I know the God in me is like oil in water - He will always cause me to rise to the top.

I don't mind taking risks to lead the pack in following Christ. I believe that the word risk is really just another word for faith. It is impossible to live by faith and not take risks. And it's impossible to move in faith without inspiring someone else to do the same.

"Now faith is the substance of things hoped for, the evidence of things not seen." -Hebrews 11:1 NIV

Living in faith is taking a risk in what you know God is going to do or has already done and walking it out until the manifestation of that thing comes to life. If acting on something without seeing it isn't a risk, I don't know what is.

I believe God has called and created leaders to be at the forefront of every sphere of influence on the earth (family, entertainment, media, education, religion, economics, and government). This will require faith in who God has called you to be, leading others through that call, and doing it out loud. Every sphere of life ought to be illuminated because of the light of the leaders that God has placed in this world. One of the biggest dangers in life and leadership is having the ability to lead but taking on this false sense of humility. We limit the influence of God on the earth by trying to hide behind this wall of humbleness, not wanting to be seen as arrogant.

We are living in a season and time in Christianity that all leaders have an assignment to exercise their God-given right and abilities to lead or to be influential on the earth. God said when you pray, you ought to say, your kingdom come, your will be done on earth as it is in heaven. God is literally holding us responsible for being influencers in the earthly realm as He is in the heavenly realm. Holding the power and reigns of the earth just as He is in heaven. The sons of God are those who are willing, by faith, to lead like God.

This is how love is made complete among us so that we will have confidence on the day of judgment: In this world, we are like Jesus. - 1 John 4:17

Did y'all see that? We are like Jesus! As He is, so are we in this world. As He leads, so do we. So how is He? Show me an instance where Jesus shied away. He never backed down from a challenge. God never closed His eyes to a cause. Wherever Jesus went, He took life head on. God never refused or ran from a fight. We ought to lead in the same way.

Do you remember the game, follow the leader? Just in case you weren't born yet, the rules were just as it sounds. You choose a leader, and everyone has to do exactly as they do. We as leaders follow our leader, Jesus Christ. This is the ultimate form of leadership. Leaders must first be led, and although leaders are correcting others, they are also being corrected.

We as leaders and children of God should be constantly growing and evolving. As you lead, grow, and as you grow, lead! Remember, leadership is like water. When it becomes stagnant, it stinks. Try to discover something new about yourself every day. The Greatest Threat to any Revolution is the absolute lack of Individual Evolution. The day you stop growing, you stop everything. A life of growth and increase, demands discipline. Show me a leader without discipline and I will show someone who is on the way to failure.

We must have discipline if we are going to live a life that properly discharges disciples. The power to lead comes from what we do in our personal life, not what we portray to do in front of others. Attempting to lead someone else in an area that we are not willing to go in ourselves is not leadership, it's manipulation. That is not what God is calling us to be about.

Leaders form healthy habits that they display out loud for others to follow. Most of us know or have heard that anything you do consistently for over 30 days becomes a habit. But we have the power to determine what those habits are, which will also determine our destiny. A habit is a useful servant but a dangerous master because we form our habits and then they form us. Think about the type of person you want to be, determine why you should inspire other people, and then decide if your daily habits are congruent with those desires.

God gives us a mandate of leadership in Matthew 28:19

Therefore, go and make disciples of all nations.

Jesus told us to go and make disciples, not go and make suggestions. If you did a quick search on the word 'make,' you would find out that it means to force against a person's will. Sometimes, we are leading people who do not have the will to go where God is taking them. People beaten down by life and circumstances need a push to get where God says they need to be. You are that push. We do not make disciples by force but by our influence and love for them.

"By love and kindness have I drawn you." (Jeremiah 31:3).

We have to be disciples to make disciples. And we have to know the love of God, to love others. If we lead people in such a way that our love and concern for them is in the forefront of what they do, then our influence will have an impact.

We must learn not to just walk the walk, but we need to learn to talk the talk of the people. All the wisdom and intelligence in the world doesn't help any if we can't communicate at a level that others understand. Leading out loud with clarity is the difference between making noise and being heard. I can reach people regardless of what level they are on. I can sit down with the elderly and talk about life and then turn around and talk to a teenager. I can even talk about life to a kindergartner. True leading out loud is coming down to a level where someone else is, and pulling them up to where you are.

If it is true that the church has a shortage of influential leaders, then it is also true that the leaders are still in the church. But we need to step forward and be seen. We need to be recognized; we need to stand tall. Everyone needs to be the best leader, the very best influencer we can be if we really believe that God's will, word, and way is right for the world today.

I believe if we are going to lead out loud, we must lead from our place of brokenness. What is brokenness? Brokenness is when God strips us of our self-sufficiency and brings us to the end of ourselves. The prodigal son finally reached a place of brokenness when He realized that everything He needed was with His Father (Luke 15:11-32). Jesus also says something similar.

"I am the vine; you are the branches. If you remain in me and I in you, you will bear much fruit; apart from me, you can do nothing." - John 15:5

The prodigal son realized He was nothing and had nothing. When we come to this realization that we are nothing outside of Christ, then we can lead out loud in a way that allows God to flow through us. Without him, I can do nothing. There are few more powerful words spoken than these. It is through Christ and with Christ that all things are possible.

Leading Out Loud Includes Mistakes

I just want to encourage those who are already leading and want to lead, that no matter what happens, you must press forward and be an example even in the mistakes and shortcomings. We have all been there; we have all sinned and come short of the glory of God (Romans 3:23).

If you were leading out loud but somewhere along the way, you fell from grace, or missed the mark, my advice to you at this time and juncture in your life is to repent.

When we mess up, we must take ownership and accountability for our faults. If we think someone else is to blame, then we can't have a heart of repentance and the first step to recovery or putting you back in your proper place is to repent. And I don't mean saying sorry, I mean to make a complete turn from that lifestyle or choice unto the direction of Christ.

Just as you led the people out loud, don't hide your acts of repentance. Make your change of heart clear and allow the world to see that you acknowledge the fact that you failed, and that you conducted yourself in a manner that displeased God. People need to know that our heart breaks when God's heart breaks, and that includes our own sin. You want all to see the love and grace of God through your acts of repentance. You want people to see how God accepts fallen leaders back into the fold.

The Father of the prodigal son was aware of His son's failure but was happy and willing to accept Him and restore Him to an even higher place than before when the son could take ownership and repent. If we are to be restored to a position of leadership, we must overcome the embarrassment and the desire to hide from our responsibilities over the fact that we squandered what God has entrusted us with. When we turn to God, we realize that under His wings, hands, and authority; we have everything we need to get back up.

When we take the time to clean up our messes, we are going to say, "I made a mistake, I tried, I have fallen." The beauty is we are yet yielding towards God when we say these things. We are going back to reestablish our trust with God and with those we lead. This is a call to those who have fallen and made mistakes; to get up! I have had my fair share of shortcomings, but I have realized that God loves me, and the love of God is far greater than my faults, my failures, and my foolishness. This isn't an excuse to make bad choices but is the grace we need to recover from them.

God loved me when I felt unlovable, forgave me when I felt unforgivable, took me back when I did everything in my power to turn Him away. Because of the great love God has shown me, I knew I could not stay in that lower state of living. We must find the humility to come to ourselves. And say as the prodigal son said "in my father's care, under his influence and leadership, there is more than enough to be successful. I thought I could do this on my own, but I can't (in the words of Mike McClure)." The prodigal son couldn't do it and neither can we. Face life head on and trust God to pick up the pieces when you fall. That is what those who lead out loud do.

Leaders Are Followers First

A skilled leader is the mature product of being a great follower. What makes an influential person a prominent leader is that they understand the benefits of being a great follower. The Bible tells us to follow those who have obtained the promise.

"We don't want you to become lazy, but to imitate those who through faith and patience inherit what has been promised." - Hebrews 6:12

There are people who have what you need and who currently are where you are trying to get to in life. We must become a follower or imitator of those who have already made it where we want to go. We do this by operating with the spirit of discernment and identifying who we should follow and sit at their feet to gain wisdom and insight for our next level. We can't always sit at a feeder position, we must also be fed. We must have people to look to, someone to pull our strings and ring our bell, people who exercise authority over us and hold us accountable.

I am blessed and fortunate that I have parents that have offered great leadership in difficult times in my life. I have siblings whom I consider my personal heroes, who I have had the joy of seeing lead through challenging times and difficult situations. I have had great men of God along the way who have offered me great leadership in times and moments of life when it was needed most. There are several really great men of God who have had such a powerful influence over my life in specific seasons that were foundation building sources of leadership for my life today.

Serving Is Leading

Everyone likes the glitz and glamour of what leading out loud looks like. We like to see the stage, and the audience that is hanging on to every word. But that is not the full picture of what true leadership is. There is some hard working, impactful people of influence that may never touch a stage or a microphone a day in their life. But they are just as much a leader as the one who does the glitz and glamour.

Leadership is about serving, giving other people what they need and living from a place of selflessness. The one thing that keeps many people from stepping into the role of leading out loud is servanthood. Jesus was the best leader there was, and He washed the feet of the disciples,

He went without eating in pursuit of winning the hearts of those in need; He gave more than He received, and He cared about the needs of others, and He even said this about serving.

"But whoever would be great among you must be your servant." - Matthew 20:26

If you can't serve others, how will you lead others? It is the heart that is found in a servant that is required in a great leader. There are leaders who don't serve, who have a position of influence because of wealth, political stance, or association. But we don't want to be just any leader. We want to be the type of leader that reflects the heart of Christ and His promotion only by the hand of God and not our own agenda.

It sounds like we have some choices to make. Are we going to lead, and if so, what kind of leader are we going to be? Remember, you are going to lead others regardless, so make sure you choose to take on the responsibility of leading seriously.

The key to leading out loud is taking advantage of the power of choice. Power of Choice means that you can decide where you want to go in life. It means that you can choose to do work that matters. It means that you can, through the choices you make, bring forth your incredible human potential. So, choose to lead, lead with all your beautiful brilliance, lead like without you, it's a wrap and all is lost. Lead out loud!

CHAPTER FIVE

LAUGH OUT LOUD

L aughing out loud is about laughing on purpose, with purpose, and for a purpose. When we laugh out loud, we do so with the intent of literally showing every viable enemy that what they are bringing against us WILL NOT WORK. Our laughter is an open display of victory to any and every adversary or enemy that dare think they have the upper hand.

"You prepare a table before me in the presence of my enemies." - Psalms 23:5

God is showing out on your behalf in the presence of your enemies, so we might as well laugh in their presence too. I don't mean laughing in the face of other people at your job, or the person moving far too slow in front of you at the grocery store. Your true enemy is the devil, and we should laugh in his face every chance we get.

I know we all love to laugh; I mean, who doesn't like a good knee-smacking, tear jerking, gasping for air, laugh? When was the last time you had a laugh like that? If you are still thinking about it, you may not be laughing out loud enough and may take life too seriously.

But life is serious! Trust me, I know. But life can get so serious that we spend more of it in the grave than we do living it. Why stress ourselves out worrying about things that we can't change or fix instead of laughing our way through to the other side.

We all should look for opportunities to laugh whole-heartedly and learn to use laughter as a tool and a weapon against the enemies of our peace and joy. Our laughter is a source of strength, allowing us to never yield to suppression, oppression, or depression, but always holding our heads high, lifted towards the hills from where our help comes because that is also where our joy comes from.

"Nehemiah said, go and enjoy choice food and sweet drinks, and send some to those who have nothing prepared. This day is holy to our Lord. Do not grieve, for the joy of the Lord is your strength." Nehemiah 8:10 NIV

I am sure we all have something or someone to grieve, whether it be a life, a relationship. Some are even grieving the loss of their old selves and have never realized this. But there is joy and laughter to be found, even now.

If you have been in church for any length of time, you have probably heard that scripture more than once, but if this is the truth, then why don't we see more joyful people? We often confuse joy with happiness. Happiness is circumstantial and depends on our current situation. If you only laugh when you are happy; you are missing out on the genuine joy that is rooted in Christ and beyond trial or tribulation. Laughter springs forth from your belly as a by-product of the joy we have in Christ Jesus and all He has accomplished on our behalf. If you aren't laughing, it's because you can't see a way out of a problem that Jesus has already solved.

Many people like to take on a 'fake it until you make it' type of joy, where you plaster a smile across your face, say you are doing good and highly favored, when you are really one comment away from snapping on someone. This isn't real, and although it may be enough to keep others at bay, it isn't doing anything for the state of your soul. God didn't create us to be fake, or to fake it. God is so good that when we focus on Him, nothing has to be fake about our joy and laughter.

We can often take life too seriously, especially as Christians. We can get so wrapped up in the rules and standards of life that we forget to just have fun and enjoy the moment. I am sure we have met that one person who won't crack a smile no matter how funny a joke is. They think everything is about being Holy, but somehow never received the memo that God included laughter in that package. Don't get me wrong, though. There is a healthy balance to be found in walking in obedience to God and having a good time enjoying life. We often see these as two separate things, but they go hand in hand together. Obedience brings pleasure to God, joy to our heart, and laughter to our lips.

Laughter is one form of God's love that transcends all barriers as everyone loves a merry laugh. It is the one thing that does not require an interpreter and is a contagious, universal language that everyone understands.

Laughter Is a Gateway

In the world of communication, a gateway is a piece of networking hardware or software used for telecommunication networks that allows data to flow from one discrete network to another.

Laughter is a gateway to life that allows information from all emotions, thoughts, concerns, decisions, and actions to cohesively work in harmony with the other through the power and authority of the joy and peace of GOD. Laughter opens our senses and perceptions to be more willing to accept our decisions, mistakes, and the circumstances we find ourselves in.

It is our laughing out loud that helps us to stay in peace; it allows us to go through life with enthusiasm and energy, knowing that everything works together for our good. We shouldn't be taking life as seriously as others, always surprised, and thrown into a tailspin with every new media announcement. Laughing out loud comes from a place of peace that knows, regardless of what is going on, you are going to win!

Your victory is imminent as long as you keep going and laughing in the enemy's face. It is knowing deep within the inner you that greater is he that is within you than he that is in the world (1 John 4:4). We are often searching for an outside force to be greater, but the greatness of God dwells on the inside of you and when you laugh, you release a war cry of victory. Laughter is confidence and an encouraging conversation with yourself that says "I got this," even when you don't feel you do.

Many people have a problem with laughing out loud because in their mind they take laughing as negative. They consider it ignoring the situation or avoiding the circumstances. I mean, how can we dare laugh when our lives are in disorder and others around us are having hard times? So, we make laughter a dissociative mechanism to accept the pains of reality. But I see it as a coping mechanism to face my realities.

This all depends on what your reality is, whether it's what your eyes see or what the word says about your situation. Laughter doesn't mean that we don't see what is happening or that we don't acknowledge our pain and the pain of others. But it does mean that we understand there is something bigger than what is happening and someone greater than the pain. No one wants to be in denial of not living in a realistic truth. Our laughter is the indicator that there is a truth higher and greater than the ones that we face.

Laughter demands deliberate demonstrative direct deliverance from all negative powers and people. In other words, if you realize you can't laugh in the presence of certain people or in specific environments, then it may be time to make some adjustments. It doesn't matter where the enemy is coming from or who he is using to get to you. We must not tolerate dissatisfaction with any action or activity against us that does not line up with the will of God. The longer we put up with things and people who rob us of our laughter, the longer we forfeit the authentic life God has planned for us.

Am I saying you need to be laughing all the time, every second of the day? Of course not, or you stand a risk of ending up in a crazy house. But you should laugh when it matters. When the enemy is trying to quiet your confession, confidence, and commitment to God, is when you should laugh the loudest.

I'm laughing because this will not kill me but only make me stronger. I am going to wait until my change comes. I don't do something crazy, fall apart, break down, and don't let the enemy break in while waiting for a breakthrough. I stand on my core belief and laugh. Someone told me when I was a youngster that I should never let my enemies see me sweat, so I replaced sweating with laughter. Now it's double trouble. Not only are you not going to see me sweat, but I am going to laugh all the way to victory.

Life can be wildly tragic, and I've had my share of tragedies. But whatever happens to me, I've learned how to keep a slightly comedic attitude. In the final analysis, I never forget to laugh. I have come across many challenges in life that I can laugh at later. This has helped me to understand that when we trust God, we can laugh amid the situation because we know we will come out fine on the other side. Laughter is an act of faith. It tells the enemy that we have no worries about what He is doing. The Bible says we will look at our troubles as waters passed by (Job 11:16). We can also see our troubles for exactly what they are during this time of experience. What we go through is temporary, fleeting, and on its way out.

Sometimes laughing out loud is literally just slowing down and seeing your situation from God's point of view. Imagine someone walking in a park compared to the view of someone above in a helicopter. Our view is very limited and circumstantial, and unless we get above what is happening in our lives, we can never laugh at it. But how do we get above it? By embracing our position in Christ. The Bible says that we are seated with Christ in heavenly places (Ephesians 2:6). That means we have a bird's eye view of our situation. And when we open our word and stand on the promises of God, we are looking at life from an aerial view that should provoke joy and laughter.

I do not intend for the laughter I speak of in this book to come from a sarcastic, sour, insincere place. To abuse the privilege of laughing actually puts one in danger of aborting the creative process that the LORD uses to birth within us what's real in heaven but not yet true concerning us on earth. Laughter plays a far greater role in our lives than many of us have come to understand.

If we abuse this gift or privilege to laugh, we tie up the hands of God to be locked up outside of His promises, which means we are not open to what heaven has for us.

Heaven says I am healed but if I lock it out, I stay sick. Heaven says I am prosperous, but if I lock it out, I stay in poverty. Sadness, depression, fear, and anxiety keep us from receiving and place us in an area of doubt, tying God's hands to defend us. Because laughter expresses faith and confidence (in my opinion). In my life, I always choose to use laughter as a weapon and sign of faith.

Laughter Changes Things

When we put sound and visuals together, they translate emotions. Nowhere is this clearer as when we wholeheartedly laugh. We hear the word of the Lord, and we see His promises, and it causes a laugh to overflow from the pit of our stomachs. Laughter to the children of God is like a roar to a lion. Everyone knows when a lion roars, they need to back up. The Bible says that we are as bold as a lion (Proverbs 28:1), so we might as well let off a roaring laugh for all to hear.

We can use laughter or laughing out Loud as a formidable kind of therapy as it can be extremely therapeutic.

A cheerful heart is good medicine... - Proverbs 17:22 NIV

Laughter literally signals the release of endorphins in your body, giving you the airy, light feeling that all is well despite what is happening. Your laughter reduces your stress and even makes your immune system stronger, aids in fighting off sickness and reducing pain in your body. There are more reasons to laugh than not.

The success of therapy and lasting change requires that the person come in contact with previously inaccessible aspects of the true feelings. The way out of trauma is by going through it (Epstein, 1994). Coming to terms with the overwhelming pain of one's past liberates dissociated feelings, and allows us to be free to laugh in areas that once made us cry.

When we assimilate the unconscious into our conscious knowledge structures, we become who we are. And who are we? We aren't our past; we aren't what happened to us or who others said we could or could not be. We are children of God, and that alone gives us reason to laugh out loud.

The key to all this is not so much laughing but one's willingness and courage to do so in the face of adversity. Your laughter is what the sling shot was to David, what the staff was to Moses, what a flag is to a war. It is our weapon, our tool, our sign of victory, our spring of joy flowing from God, our contagious communication, that goes beyond language barriers, and our war cry. Laugh often, laugh hard, and laugh intentionally. Laugh so hard that you make the enemy feel stupid and confused for meddling with you. Laugh because you know the battle is not yours and Jesus has already won.

CHAPTER SIX
LEND OUT LOUD

So, this last chapter is no surprise to anyone that knows Mike McClure or just about any McClure of my blood. The McClure's are flat out, point blank, unapologetic, undaunted lenders, as the scripture calls us, more commonly known as Givers.

I grew up around givers, constantly being exposed to what it means to give. My siblings and I, from an early age, watched and learned from our mom the beauty and blessings of being gracious to others. When I lived in the projects of Collegeville in Birmingham Alabama... I was Po... We didn't get the other OR of Poor out of layaway.

I still remember when my mom would help the other kids by handing out lunches from our back door, ensuring all the kids in the area had food to take to school. My mom didn't hand out lunches because we were rich; she gave despite our own lack because she had the heart of a giver and faith in God. And because of this faith in God, it also gave us passion for God and compassion for people.

I didn't realize it then, but my exposure to the generosity of my mother was the beginning of a compassionate heart towards others and the foundation of a blessed life. It was my mom's own sacrifice of both time and money that she not only invested in the life of someone else, but into the kingdom of God. Through her giving, she impacted all those who were there as a witness to her compassion.

It really all comes down to that one word. COMPAS-SION.

The word compassion was used several times in the life of Jesus and was always concluded by Him helping to meet the needs of others. Because the thing about compassion is that it compels you to act. Feeling sorry for someone is merely an emotional response to the plight of another individual. But compassion will press upon your heart in such a way, that you MUST do something.

This same compassion lives in you and me, because that is where Jesus lives. God is still feeling compelled to help people, and He is doing it through our lives and our pockets, if we will allow Him to, that is.

God has been gracious to us all, and I just like my mother, want to live a life of being gracious to others by lending out loud. The word gracious means as a believer to show extreme kindness, generosity, and favor (I must warn you right here that most of the definitions I use for words I admittedly create myself). These are all qualities that begin and end with God, being found and developed through our relationship with Him.

The more time we spend with God and His word, the more we embody who He is. WE LEND OUT LOUD!!!! Not for show, but because it's born within us from birth. We inherited the Spirit of generosity and gratefulness. It doesn't matter who raised you, or what type of environment you grew up in, whether it was in poverty or wealth.

When we were born again, we took on a new family and a spirit that cares about others.

Generosity is a fruit of God's grace, something that an individual should feel compelled to do from their own hearts. While in one way, this understanding liberates us from any legalism around giving, it simultaneously heightens our expectations for giving. Because generosity flows from the heart and it is a tangible way of expressing and exposing the condition of the heart.

Generosity should be a defining characteristic of not only the McClure's but of all believers of every ethnos because GOD is generous. The Father gave His Son.

What are you giving?

Getting Over Ourselves

We can't lend out loud if we don't first get over ourselves and see beyond our own point of need. Self - centeredness and a poverty mindset will always keep us from giving and that is because they both go hand in hand. Being self-centered prohibits us from putting someone else's needs above our own. Self-centeredness will cause you to believe that what belongs to you is for you and you alone, creating the unwillingness to share it with someone else.

Poverty is self-centeredness at its finest. When you are broke, you can't see beyond your own bills, so it keeps you in a repetitive cycle of poverty. We can get so deep in self-centeredness that we don't realize stepping out and giving in faith can be a way out. But I will just let the word tell you about it.

"One person gives freely, yet gains even more; another withholds unduly, but comes to poverty." – Proverbs 11:24 NIV

Remember this also: "Whoever sows sparingly will also reap sparingly, and whoever sows generously will also reap generously." – 2 Corinthians 9:6 NIV

"The stingy are eager to get rich and are unaware that poverty awaits them." – Proverbs 28:22

I think it is interesting that giving causes us to have more, but withholding will cause us to have less. The concept and foundational truth of giving is the opposite of how the world functions. If you want money, you must save it, but God says if you give, you will have more. Leave it to God to use the simple things to confound the wise.

Lending out loud is giving despite your own lack and allowing your love to be at the forefront in the midst of your own want and circumstances. We will always be in need or desire something. If we allow our desires to be the driving force of whether we are givers, we will never lend out loud. Giving is the opposite of what they have taught many of us to do or how society says we should live, but God is a giver and just as I was a natural giver because of my mother, we should all be natural givers because of our heavenly Father.

Giving isn't about helping others or paying tithes once everything in your life is perfect. Many people may not believe this, but if you can't be a giver when you have less money, it will be harder to give when you have more. As a matter of fact, I would like to ask you a question really quick.

Can God trust you with poverty? Can God trust you with trouble? Can God trust you through lack?

Having everything picture perfect will never work because there will always be a new thing to add to our list and a situation that requires our financial attention.

When we give of what we have, it helps us to keep our eyes and hearts off ourselves and onto God. I am sure you may wonder how giving what we have worked hard for equates to keeping our eyes on God. I'll tell you how.

Well, because the Bible says that where our treasure is, there will our heart be also, and not the other way around (Matthew 6:21). Just think about it; you are more than just financially invested in what you use your money towards. When you buy new clothes, you are emotionally invested in the excitement, physically invested in the wearing of the clothes. It may even change your mood and alter the way you feel about yourself. Or even stocks. You watch them like a hawk and study trends and investment information.

Because what happens to your money is important and the way you feel about it affects you.

When you give to someone in need or to your local church through tithes and offering, you are giving into God's kingdom. No, you are not walking up to the throne of God and handing Him money, but you are fulfilling His will in the earth through your giving. And just like with the new clothes or stock investments, you are involving yourself in Kingdom living.

One of the biggest issues with giving is mentality, the way we view money and the way we view God concerning money. When we see God from the right perspective and have an identity that is rooted in Him, our perception of money will change. Not overnight, but the more you grow in understanding, the more your actions will come into alignment.

Our father in heaven owns everything, even the cattle on a thousand hills (Psalms 50:7). If you are a Christian, then you are a joint heir with Christ, taking ownership by faith of all that belongs to you. Take hold of what you have in Christ and give by faith. It is the revolving cycle of giving that blesses everyone involved. I bless God when I give; I bless the person receiving, and then God blesses me. As you can see, everyone is a winner.

Understand who you are by spending time with God. You and God will build a rapport with one another, which will become an intimate exchange that will have you moving, spending, living, and giving in new ways.

There are five questions that helped me shape my life and have been a constant reminder of my personal and spiritual formation.

1.What do you want? God has planted a desire in your heart, which can often be found when you consider who you see yourself being and what you see yourself doing.

2. How bad do you want it? You must be willing to be self-disciplined, make yourself uncomfortable, and welcome change in order to see change.

3. Is the thing you want the thing that God wants for you? Our ways and thoughts do not always line up with God which is why we must commit them to Him so God can bring them in line with His plans.

4. What are you willing to give or sow in order to have it? Seeds always represent future blessing.

5. Are you willing to proclaim it before you hold it in your hand? The righteous live by faith and those who plan on receiving must speak by faith.

God always forms before He fills, and we must embrace being formed into His likeness. The bridge between where we are, and our preferred destination is our formation because our outward prosperity is connected to our inward growth. Grow in God, act like God, and receive from God.

Between You and God

Lending aka giving out loud, isn't about giving for anyone else to see, but giving unto God. I know we like to pull out our cameras and get ready for a post when we do something generous, but the only reward we receive in seeking man's attention is the attention they give us, forfeiting our heavenly reward. Giving differs from the other areas of life that we want to live freely and openly before others. God has a heavenly reward for us when our generosity comes from a pure heart void of attention-seeking ambition. I would take a heavenly reward any day over the praise of men.

"But when you give to the needy, do not let your left hand know what your right hand is doing." -Matthew 6:3 NIV

With God, it is about more than our actions; it is the intent that drives the action. Lending out loud is more about our heart posture. It has more to do with why we are giving than who we are giving to, and who saw us. The widow woman in the book of Luke knows all about giving from the heart.

And He looked up and saw the rich putting their gifts into the treasury, and He saw also a certain poor widow putting in two mites. So, he said, "Truly I say to you that this poor widow has put in more than all; for all these out of their abundance have put in offerings for God, but she out of her poverty put in all likelihood that she had." -Luke 21:1-4

This woman was poor, and not what we consider poor, where you still have updated electronics and new cars but don't have any money left over. No... she was PO...There were those who had money giving out of the abundance of wealth and Jesus said that she had put in more than them all. Now that is lending out loud!!

When we give from the heart, our lending becomes a tool, not only a tool, but a weapon. In our giving, we use money as a weapon to fight against the power of darkness and take something that the world often uses for evil and corruption to build the kingdom of heaven. We give because we got it to give! Some of you may think about your bank account saying, "Do we?" Absolutely, if you believe that what belongs to your father belongs to you, then you got it!

"Now he who supplies seed to the sower and bread for food will also supply and increase your store of seed and enlarge the harvest of your righteousness." - 2 Corinthians 9:10

This is the original two for one special. God will give you seed to sow and food to eat. But it says He gives seed to the Sower. God distinguished a difference between sowing and eating, so we understand He meets our personal needs and makes sure we are sowing in the lives of others. Not only that, but the scripture says He increases our seed, and another version says that God multiplies the seed sown, which means an increased harvest!

To many, the concept of giving will only make sense through faith, and I pray God gives you the ears to hear and the eyes to see. We can all start giving from right where we are, and God will honor your lending out loud.

Maybe reading this chapter has created in you the desire to give but you feel you have nothing to give with. I believe God will help you get the ball rolling if you will only ask him: "Father, your word says that you will give seed to the Sower. I want to be a sower but I don't have any seed. I am asking you for seed, so that I may give unto your kingdom. I want to lend out loud"

Don't worry about God doing His part. He will always act according to His word, but when He does, make sure you are faithful to sow the seed.

Others may try to make you feel you are being naïve by giving and that you are allowing the church to walk over or take advantage of you. And although these things have happened, leaving a nasty taste in the mouths of some who genuinely want to lend out loud, it does not have to be the truth.

God called us to be givers, not ignorant! We can give with discernment; we can judge a situation and even ask God for guidance on where to give and how to give. We do not want to sow our financial seed into places that do not sincerely have the heart of God and people who will allow money to be a hindrance instead of a help. Although God wants us to give, He wants to sow into good ground.

Not every ministry is for God, nor does everyone have good intentions. It is up to us to use wisdom and discernment in giving.

Giving is Good

"One who is gracious to a poor man lends to the Lord, And He will repay him for his good deed." - Proverbs 19:17 NASB

According to scripture, one's generosity and extreme kindness and desire to show favor to others is defined by GOD as a good deed! Good!! We can't really talk about good deeds and giving without defining exactly what good means.

1. Good is the archenemy of evil!

Because good opposes evil, you can usually find a hater or someone trying to speak evil against someone doing good.

2. Good is head and shoulders above average.

Average is good in the world's eyes, but good is satisfaction in the eyes of God. When God created the world, he looked at all he had done and called it good. So, when we think about the word good, we must put it in its proper place.

3.Good opposes all that displeases GOD.

What God considers good will never make sense to the natural mind. But don't let that deter you from lending out loud, from giving out of a pure heart and seeing God bless you in a way that only He can.

As creatures of THE LORD, we are to be creative, yet we are never to be satisfied with creating anything that's not good. When we venture out of creating goodness, we pervert the gift of creation itself, which simply means to alter something from its original intent. God's intent for creation was good and for us as children to create good like our heavenly Father. Giving allows us to create good in so many ways which would allow God's goodness to overflow into our lives.

In my opinion, good is the starting point of greatness, greatness is the continual search for excellence, and excellence is the foundation of significance.

We see significance in Cornelius the Centurion, in the book of Acts.

"And fixing his gaze on him and being much alarmed, he said, "What is it, Lord?" And he said to him, 'Your prayers and alms have ascended as a memorial before God.'" - Acts 10:4 NASB

WOW! Not just his prayers, but his alms (his giving) came up before GOD. It gets no more significant than that.

God is not overlooking your giving, so don't let your current situation convince you that God does not see the seeds you have sown. You will reap your harvest in due time and everything you gave will be worth the sacrifice, not only in God blessing you, but in you being a blessing in the life of another.

As you learn to Lend out Loud, never fall prey to the CRISIS of COMPARISON or the PERILS of PERFORM-ANCE. Many times, what impresses imprisons. We can become impressed with the giving lifestyle of someone else that we become in bondage to giving as a desire of living a certain lifestyle instead of living like God.

Do not allow others to make you feel guilty about your giving, that you are not giving enough. Give cheerfully from your heart because God loves a cheerful giver (2 Corinthians 9:7).

Our actions speak for us in ways that our words never can. Communicate through your giving what's in your heart but more importantly, what's in GOD'S heart concerning you. When we are faithful to walk in the truth and financial principles of the word, we allow Jesus to come into our situations.

The presence of Jesus always announces the possibility of divine intervention. Even in times of not enough, our giving will cause God to intervene with supernatural provision as He did with Elijah and the widow woman. Elijah asked that she give her some food, but she didn't have enough. Because of her obedience, God provided for her and her family supernaturally until the famine was over.

Elijah said to her, "Don't be afraid. Go home and do as you have said. But first make a small loaf of bread for me from what you have and bring it to me and then make something for yourself and your son. For this is what the Lord, the God of Israel, says: 'The jar of flour will not be used up and the jug of oil will not run dry until the day the Lord sends rain on the land." -1 Kings 17:13-14

What amazes me so much about this miracle is not that God never allowed her barrel of meal to overflow, but He did ensure that it never ran out.

I said it before, and I will say it again. God will always do His part. We must make sure that we do ours. This isn't about another preacher trying to talk you into giving to his ministry. This is about developing a relationship with God and allowing Him to create His same desires in your heart.

If you were not a giver before reading this chapter, you may not be one after it is over. But I guarantee if you submit that area of your life to God, that you will be compelled to lend out loud because of the way God is moving on you to help others. If you dare to lend out loud, prepare to see your life change, and if you were already doing it, keep up the good work! Let's change our world by showing it what true lending out loud looks like.

Not only lending, but living, loving, learning, leading, and laughing out loud. The world isn't getting any less crazy, and it needs you and me to take these life lessons and allow them to cause us to stand up and take our position.

During these times, what are you called to do, who are you called to be, what are you called to say, and what are you called to give? There is an impact that is destined to be made on the world through you, and it starts with knowing who you are and being who you are with no turning back. Are you ready? The greatest version of you is waiting!

AFTERWORD

After reading through the pages of this book, I hope and pray that your perspective on life has been altered. I pray that now you have been liberated and launched into a whole new way of living your best life in Christ. Whatever you choose to be or do, please at all cost, be YOU!

I'm Mike McClure and I approve this message. Peace!!

www.ingramcontent.com/pod-product-compliance
Lightning Source LLC
Chambersburg PA
CBHW071018120626
46546CB00003B/1152